CW00685363

DOMESTIC IMPERIALISM

NINE REASONS
I LEFT PROGRESSIVISM

KEITH KNIGHT

The
LIBERTARIAN
INSTITUTE

DOMESTIC IMPERIALISM

NINE REASONS
I LEFT PROGRESSIVISM

KEITH KNIGHT

Domestic Imperialism:
Nine Reasons I Left Progressivism

Published in the United States of America by

The Libertarian Institute
612 W. 34th St.
Austin, TX 78705

LibertarianInstitute.org

ISBN 13: 979-8-9884031-2-8

To Carey Wedler, for rejecting double standards

Table of Contents

Introduction

Consider these two organizations. Which one sounds more compassionate?

Organization X offers people food in exchange for money. When people refuse to exchange money for Organization X's food, Organization X uses their own money to market their products and reinvest in facilities which entice customers to shop there. If customers refuse to buy food from Organization X, Organization X will go out of business.

Organization Q produces food. Organization Q claims that since food is necessary for life and a healthy populace, people should be forced to chip in for Organization Q's costs. Those who do not pay will be put in jail by employees of Organization Q, and if you resist Organization Q's employees, the employees have the right to shoot you in defense of their own lives.

Which organization sounds *more* compassionate? Which organization would you prefer to interact with?

Governments provide many things, such as security, schools, intelligence gathering, and poverty assistance programs, but none of these are defining characteristics of governments. They can be provided by many non-government actors in society, and historically, they have been.[1]

What makes government a unique institution in society is its widely recognized right to achieve its ends via threats of violence against non-aggressors.

This is why you would go to jail for trying to "tax" someone's income, or if you attempted to "regulate" the commercial interactions of strangers, or "declared war" on one of your foes.

Hence, governmental organizations are more like Organization Q, and organizations in the free market are more like Organization X.

I became a Progressive when I thought that Progressivism meant being compassionate. I stopped being a Progressive when I realized that putting massive obligations on strangers through government coercion was not compassion.

While Progressives assume that they have a monopoly on compassion, the reality is that compassion can still arise even in the absence of state coercion.

This book will focus on Progressive ideas which dominate universities, K-12 teaching, the corporate press, governments, corporate advertising campaigns, human resource departments, and Hollywood.

Most of the people in these areas advocate Progressive ideas such as state welfare, state schooling, antitrust legislation, state involvement in healthcare, state involvement in retirement planning, state regulation of commerce, and the belief that the existence of disparities in outcomes is ample evidence of discrimination.[2]

Three things to know before moving forward:

• The primary assumption behind Progressivism: Government is the central caretaker in society when it comes to solving social and individual problems.

• In America, both Republican President Theodore Roosevelt and Democratic President Woodrow Wilson were considered "Progressives," showing that the fundamental assumptions within this worldview exist across party lines. This is why whenever "small government" Republicans have been in power, they have never shrunk, on net, the size or scope of the federal government.[3]

• The Progressive mentality tends to assume that inequality and poverty are unnatural and the result of bad actors, while equality and wealth are easily achievable with the right amount of political power.

In a world where Progressive assumptions rule general public opinion, I wanted to write this short book explaining why the Progressive worldview should be rejected and the free market worldview should be embraced instead.

Terms

Voluntaryism
The moral position which maintains that no peaceful person can justly be submitted to the control of others, in the absence of his or her own consent.

Libertarianism
The moral position which maintains that it is illegitimate to initiate aggression against non-aggressors.

Anarchy
From the Greek prefix *an*, "without, in the absence of" and the Greek noun *archon*, "master, ruler." *Anarchy* does not mean "without rules"; it literally means "without rulers, without masters."

Communism
The abolition of private property.

Socialism
The institutionalized interference with, or aggression against, private property and private property claims.

Capitalism
A social system based on the explicit recognition of private property, and non-aggressive contractual exchanges between private property owners.

Free Market
A summary description of all voluntary exchanges that take place in a given economic environment.

Original Appropriation
A process by which previously unowned natural resources, particularly land, become the property of a person or group of persons.

Contract
Consensual title transfer between two or more parties.

Exchange
A voluntary interaction between two individuals in which both forfeit ownership of an object to the other, to the benefit of both.

Economics

The study of purposeful behavior applied to the use of scarce resources which have alternative uses.

Scarcity/Scarce
Limited with respect to the ends that resources could possibly serve.

Property
A term describing anything over which a party has legal title, affording owners certain enforceable rights over said scarce resources.

Political Authority
The hypothesized moral property in virtue of which governments may coerce people in certain ways not permitted to anyone else and in virtue of which citizens must obey governments in situations in which they would not be obligated to obey anyone else.

Non-Aggression Principle (NAP)
An ethical stance which asserts that initiating aggression is inherently illegitimate.

Aggression
The initiation of physical force against persons or property, the threat of such, or fraud upon persons or their property. In contrast to pacifism, the non-aggression principle does not preclude violent self-defense. The principle is a deontological (or rule-based) ethical stance.

Self-Ownership
Also known as "sovereignty of the individual" or "individual sovereignty"; the concept of property in one's own person, expressed as the moral or natural right of a person to have bodily integrity and be the exclusive controller of his or her own body and life.

Ownership
The recognized right of one party to exclude another from scarce resources.

State
That organization in society which attempts to maintain a monopoly of the use of force and violence in a given territorial area; in particular, it is the only organization in society that obtains its revenue not by voluntary contribution or payment for services rendered, but by coercion.

1. Arbitrary Divides

On June 12, 2016, Omar Mateen murdered 49 people and wounded 53 at the Pulse nightclub in Orlando, Florida. While inside Pulse, Mateen called the police to admit to the terrorist act in hopes of amplifying his motives.[4]

Here is how then-President Barack Obama* addressed this tragedy four days later:

> This was an attack on the LGBT community. Americans were targeted because we're a country that has learned to welcome everyone, no matter who you are or who you love. And hatred towards people because of sexual orientation, regardless of where it comes from, is a betrayal of what's best in us.[5]

Here are the actual words spoken by Mateen in his phone call with police on the night of the massacre:

> You have to tell America to stop bombing Syria and Iraq. They are killing a lot of innocent people. What am I to do here when my people are getting killed over there? You get what I'm saying?...
>
> You need to stop the U.S. air strikes. They need to stop the U.S. air strikes, okay?...
>
> They need to stop the U.S. air strikes. You have to tell the U.S. government to stop bombing. They are killing too many children. They are killing too many women, okay?...
>
> I feel the pain of the people getting killed in Syria and Iraq... They need to stop bombing Syria and Iraq. The U.S. is collaborating with Russia, and they are killing innocent women and children, okay?...
>
> The air strikes need to stop, and stop collaborating with Russia. Okay?... Tell — tell the fucking — the air strikes need to stop... You see, now you feel, now you feel how it is, now you feel how it is.[6]

Barack Obama took what was clearly a response to the U.S. government's foreign policy as an opportunity to place focus on the arbitrary demographic of the victims' sexual orientation. He didn't say, "This was an attack on young people," even though most victims were young. He didn't say, "This was an attack on Floridians," even though the attack occurred in Florida.

---

* Barack Obama was elected in 2008 on a Progressive platform opposing imperialist wars, increasing wealth and opportunities for the economically vulnerable through schooling and healthcare, and a plan to increase regulation in the financial sector.

A sane response would have been: "This tragedy shows us the human cost of our government's violence against innocent people abroad. As Americans, we must reject the use of violence against innocent people to achieve our goals as a nation, regardless of country, gender, nationality, or sexual orientation. We must constantly have a policy, both foreign and domestic, which embraces life, liberty, and the peaceful pursuit of happiness."

To clarify, in 2016, the year of the Pulse massacre, the United States government dropped 24,287 bombs on Iraq and Syria, according to the Council on Foreign Relations.[7]

The use of arbitrary divides involves separating people based on accidents of birth or irrelevant personal attributes, as opposed to actions they as individuals choose to engage in. Here are some arbitrary group identities commonly used by Progressives to divide people of goodwill:

• Male vs. Female

• Rich vs. Poor

• Russian vs. American

• Straight vs. Gay

• Black vs. White

Two more examples illustrate this issue, first from CNN in an article titled, "US Black-White Inequality in 4 Charts."[8] Second, Congresswoman Alexandria Ocasio-Cortez's speech combating the "Gender Pay Gap."[9]

The implicit assumption is that the existence of inequality is the result of discrimination and the state must coercively step in and mandate equality between groups. Here are some disparities in America that the article and the speech both conveniently neglect to mention:

• How many hours men work annually compared to women.[10]

• Which fields men tend to study compared to those which women tend to study (Engineering? Communications?) and how ambitiously they studied.[11]

• Black immigrants to America earn more than U.S.-born blacks.[12]

• Married men earn more than unmarried men.[13]

• The State Wage Gap: Maryland vs. Mississippi Median Income.[14]

• Age Wage Gap: Older men earn more than younger men.[15]

• Indian Americans and Asian Americans earn more than White Americans.[16]

• Most homeless people are men.[17]

• Men are 10 times more likely to die on the job.[18]

• Men are roughly 50% of the American population, but 95% of those killed by police.[19]

• Women are roughly 50% of the American population, but 89% of the elementary school teachers.[20]

• Female OnlyFans creators earn 78% more than their male counterparts.[21]

• One Kenyan tribe (the Kalenjin) produce the world's best Olympic runners.[22]

• 80% of California doughnut shops are owned by Cambodians.[23]

The reality is that disparities in outcomes are all around us and are not *only* the result of unjust discrimination. Progressives seemingly cherry-pick certain disparities to create division among populations so that they can have an enemy, thereby justifying their desire to rule over others.

Focusing on disparities also distracts from focusing on the principle at hand. Progressives often will oppose the "War on Drugs," for example, on the grounds that certain demographics are disproportionately targeted for drug arrests. But this assumes that the state has the right to imprison people for victimless crimes, so all that police need to do is arrest more people at a rate proportional to each demographic. According to the Selective Service System, all men ages 18–26 must register for "the draft." One way to approach this is to say that forced labor is immoral. Another is to say that this is sexist and discriminatory; therefore, women too must be forced to perform labor against their will.

"The Profit Motive" is another arbitrary divide Progressives use. Every time a person acts, he is using scarce resources (time, effort, money, products, etc.) at his disposal in an attempt to improve his situation. This is the nature of *Homo economicus*. Every second you spend reading, you're not sleeping or hiking; for every dollar you spend on coffee, it's one less dollar you can spend on clothing. The Progressive takes this universal reality of trade-offs and then pins it uniquely on the free market.

Do politicians not profit from television appearances and from large crowds cheering their names? Setting aside psychic profit, politicians aren't exactly unpaid volunteers, with most of them having net worths much higher than those of their constituents. Soldiers, teachers, and police officers are also profit-seekers as opposed to unpaid volunteers or people who don't reap any mental or social status benefits from their employment. Everyone is trying to maximize "profit" at every moment of every day.

Actor Sean Penn recently used the example of "when the police show up to protect Grandma, they don't make her put down a credit card," insinuating that the government exudes generosity while the free market is greedy. What happens when Grandma doesn't pay sales tax, property tax, or income tax? Does the government call her and say, "Ms. Grandma, we noticed you didn't chip in this year to the Internal Revenue Service… Are you unhappy with our services? Please reconsider being our customer"? Of course not. The state will imprison people for not giving them money, a method far greedier than offering a service voluntarily.

It's also worth noting how the voluntary profit incentive encourages goodwill among people. Almost every time I purchase a good or service in the private sector, the employees will thank me for shopping at their store. However, after having been a net taxpayer for 11 years, I have never once been thanked by a police officer, soldier, teacher, or politician.

This constant attempt to divide people of goodwill based on arbitrary attributes is what makes Progressivism such an insidious ideology.

Instead of separating heroes from villains based on income or accidents of birth as Progressivism does, people should be divided based on whose behavior is peaceful, honest, and cooperative in opposition to people whose behavior is violent, fraudulent, and parasitic.

2. The Unavoidable Contradiction

Progressives' central criticism of the free market is that such a system would lead to monopolies, where one person or group dominates an industry, resulting in higher prices and lower quality than what would exist under a more competitive situation.

The Progressive then advocates that the government monopolize taxation, business licensing, the justice system, guns, police, military, compulsory schooling, and the money supply.

Consider the blatant double standard when it comes to the word *contract*, which usually implies that I will do X for you in exchange for Y.

When you don't pay taxes, you are denounced for supposedly not upholding your end of the "social contract," and this justifies putting you in jail. However, what if the state doesn't uphold its end of the social contract and fails to keep you safe? Do politicians go to jail? Do you no longer have a legal obligation to obey arbitrary legislation or pay taxes?

Such a contradiction becomes crystal clear when we hear Progressives demanding that "assault weapons" be banned. To ban such a product would mean that no person could legally own it, even though the Progressive seems to have no problem with the American or Ukrainian military handling such "assault weapons." Even after all of the atrocities committed by governments throughout history, the Progressive still advocates government supremacy and the monopolization of "assault weapons."

Testing the Theory

Were Donald Trump and George W. Bush bigger threats to humanity as private citizens or as public officials?

According to Progressivism, the private sector is predatory and selfish, while the public sector is beneficial and cooperative.

The primary way to falsify this theory would be to take the very same person (or group of people) and see the results he produces in the private sector and the political sector.

In the private sector, Donald Trump and George W. Bush didn't have the ability to issue taxes on the income of strangers, nor were they able to regulate exchanges others were voluntarily engaged in. Furthermore, they also could not bomb civilians with impunity, under the guise of "national defense."

How many mass murder campaigns (often called "wars") will governments have to be involved in before Progressives admit that the state is the very threat to society that they claim to be protecting us from?

Progressives will claim that the current government has been captured by corporations, and so they shouldn't have to take any blame for state atrocities, while they advocate that the state should increase taxes and regulatory powers.

Imagine a free market advocate saying, "The free market will work very well; except the problem is all the current CEOs of companies are corrupt." While Progressives like Sam Seder frequently call free market advocates "utopians," it is Progressivism which is as utopian as ideologies can get.

Free market advocates recognize that humans are self-interested. Every time a Progressive watches TV, relaxes, or reads a book instead of building homes in Sierra Leone, he proves this point. The difference is that the free market harmonizes self-interest so as to recognize the legitimacy only of transactions which occur if all parties involved believe that they will be better off after the exchange. Within the free market aspects of society, no one can get a second of your time or a penny out of your pocket unless you voluntarily give it to him. Governments face no such check and balance.

Even major companies, such as Kodak, Sears, Sam Goody, Pan Am, A&P Grocery, Myspace, Borders, and Blockbuster, have gone bankrupt or out of business because they didn't meet consumer demand. Compare the companies listed in the *Fortune* 500 in 1955 to those listed in 2016: only 12 percent of the companies remain.[24] Far from "the rich stay rich," we constantly see consumers choosing to allocate their dollars away from companies — even the industry leaders — that don't meet consumer demand.

Domestic vs. Foreign Economic Regulation

When Progressives see Cubans risking their lives to get to America, they will frequently blame U.S. "sanctions" for the difficult lives of Cubans. Yet, they advocate that the very same government impose trade restrictions and economic regulations on its domestic population.

In the case of Cuba, a 1960 State Department memorandum titled "The Decline and Fall of Castro," authored by Deputy Assistant Secretary of State for Inter-American Affairs Lestor Mallory, describes the intention behind the policy of economic sanctions. In the memo, Mallory proposes making "the greatest inroads in denying money and supplies to Cuba, to decrease monetary and real wages, to bring about hunger, desperation, and overthrow of government."[25] Any third party coercively intervening in voluntary economic transactions is unjustifiable, regardless of the geographical distance between them.

The coercer will almost always say that his coercion is for the greater good of society. Even the concept of slavery was not exempt from these greater good justifications:

> Defenders of slavery argued that the sudden end to the slave economy would have had a profound and killing economic impact in the South where reliance on slave labor was the foundation of their economy. The cotton economy would collapse. The tobacco crop would dry in the fields. Rice would cease being profitable.

> Defenders of slavery argued that if all the slaves were freed, there would be widespread unemployment and chaos. This would lead to uprisings, bloodshed, and anarchy. They pointed to the mob's "rule of terror" during the French Revolution and argued for the continuation of the status quo, which was providing for affluence and stability for the slaveholding class and for all free people who enjoyed the bounty of the slave society.

> Defenders of slavery argued that slavery had existed throughout history and was the natural state of mankind. The Greeks had slaves, the Romans had slaves, and the English had slavery until very recently.[26]

All of this is to show that the very criticism Progressives have of the voluntary sector seldom applies to it, while it almost universally applies to the state.

An example of the ignorance undergirding the Progressive understanding of government can be seen in the "Defund and Abolish the Police" movement that took place in the United States in 2020.

Forget how polls show that many poor Americans want *more* police actively patrolling in order to discourage both violent and property crime. Everything that the Progressive advocates implies police action — if you don't obey these regulations, the police will put you in jail, or shoot you if you resist.

Without police, how can the state collect trillions of tax dollars every year to fund the countless and growing programs Progressives advocate? Without a state police force, who will confiscate guns from the citizens? Without a police force, who will coercively impose business regulations or occupational licensing?

The Progressive has fallen for the state's great magic trick — to make the violence that the state relies on for its very existence invisible.

Jehovah's Witnesses get a bad rap for going door to door and guilting people into giving them money and attention. I admire those who are willing to take their time peacefully to go out and give people arguments about what they believe and why. Aristotle allegedly said, "It is the mark of an educated mind to be able to entertain a thought without accepting it." So I keep that in mind and frequently will hear these people out.

There are very important implications in the actions of the Witnesses. They claim to believe that if I do not join their organization in some fashion, I could be facing an eternity in Hell. Yet, they still respect my freedom of choice to take such a steep risk. The conversions they have are voluntary, the bibles they hand out are voluntarily funded, church attendance is voluntary, and proselytizing is voluntary, because they respect my freedom of choice.

Progressives, on the other hand, will advocate that the police come to your house and put you in a jail cell — and shoot you if you resist — if you do not chip in for their pet projects under the guise of "taxation."

This is why those who claim that "the state is a tool which can be used for ill or good" are misguided. A "tool" implies neutrality, whereas a state necessarily means that some people have the right to coerce others in situations where non-state actors would have no such right.

3. Consent of the Governed & Gay Marriage

Progressives will tend to favor Democracy as opposed to Monarchy under the justification that under Democracy, we are ruled by "the consent of the governed."

This is clearly fallacious. Government officials have the recognized right to coerce the citizens into doing certain things, and no citizen has the recognized right to coerce government officials. Clearly, these are two distinct and separate groups of people, not a collective "we." If you do not have the right to issue taxes or regulations on others, you cannot justly delegate that right to politicians.

In the 1860s, abolitionist and entrepreneur Lysander Spooner addressed this issue in *No Treason: The Constitution of No Authority*. To summarize: No person alive signed the Constitutional form of government. In 1789, the year in which the Constitution went into effect, there were approximately 3.9 million Americans. Not everyone was consulted, nor could everyone vote. Even if everyone voted in agreement with the document at the time, that in no way would bind future generations.

Which kind of organization has the right to claim to represent you even when you explicitly denounce them and never partook in any quid pro quo agreement?

When 94-year-old Geraldine Tyler (allegedly) didn't pay property taxes to the State of Minnesota and the state seized her house, was she really consenting to the seizure?[27]

The specifics of the above example are not important. The importance lies in recognizing that a state is necessarily in conflict with the consent of the citizenry. If it were a consensual arrangement, then the state would just be a regular organization, possessing no extra rights over anyone else.

Where did Progressives get it right? Having a genuine reason for supporting something means consistently finding the universals within the particular.

The topic of gay marriage — the state granting same-sex adult couples to have the equally recognized rights as heterosexual couples to marry — was a central focus for Progressives roughly a decade ago. It was a major

Progressive victory to legalize gay marriage in a predominantly Christian country.

This was justified from many different standpoints, among them:

• They are adults, and they can do what they want with their lives.

• Straight people can get married, so gay couples should be able to as well.

• Their bodies, their choice.

• Your personal opinions shouldn't stop other people from pursuing their happiness.

• It's such a small thing for straights to live with gay marriage, but for the gay couple, it's a matter of happiness or misery, acceptance or rejection.

• Yes, gay couples can't reproduce, but what about couples who are infertile or decide not to have children?

• All bad things that can happen in a gay marriage can also happen in a straight marriage, and those shouldn't be illegal.

All it took for me to leave Progressivism was for me to take this principle of free association between consenting adults and apply it consistently to the economic realm.

Free association (and disassociation) is central to civilization, since no one does anything by himself. You may read a book while alone, for example, but you didn't write the book. The author didn't create the ink on the pages. The ink producer didn't chop down the trees to make the paper. The tools used to chop down trees were not created by the lumberjack. The author didn't invent the words in the English language. You didn't invent the light bulb, which lights the room allowing you to read.

This proper understanding of the cooperation within an economy illustrates the complex web of interactions that goes into everything that exists. The false dichotomy is: "There are things we do alone, and things we do together." The genuine dichotomy is that, because we are always cooperating, are the parties involved doing so *voluntarily*, or is one party *coercing* another?

4. Government Failure

One of the primary Progressive arguments against free markets is the "market failure" objection. It claims that markets suffer from:

- Imperfect knowledge (knowledge asymmetry)
- Imperfect competition (dog-eat-dog mentalities)
- Externalities
- Short-sightedness
- Greed

The problem with every single one of these criticisms is that it also applies to politicians, government officials, and voters.

Moreover, because governments by definition do not face competition and people cannot voluntarily opt out of funding them, governments tend to amplify these shortcomings.

Take each example individually:

Imperfect Knowledge: Are all voters equally informed? Are all politicians equally informed? Do those with top-secret security clearances have equal information to you or me about how the government operates? Nine Ivy League-trained Supreme Court Justices do not even agree on how to interpret the Constitution, let alone all of the laws and regulations passed at the federal, state, and local level.

Imperfect competition: Under a process of Democratic voting, do good-looking candidates and ugly candidates compete on an unbiased equal playing field? Do all celebrities and cultural figures abstain from swaying the competition for more votes for a given candidate? Are demagogues and truth-tellers evaluated equally by the masses of voters? Every two years in America, there is a highly competitive, slanderous, deceptive advertising competition to see which governor, senator, mayor, or congressman can get the most votes. It's also worth mentioning that voters are frequently understood to be ignorant on political topics, considering how much time it takes to get informed and in the end they each only get one vote among thousands or millions, unlikely to affect the outcome.

Externalities: An externality is said to exist when Person X and Person Y engage in an exchange for which Person Z has to bear the cost. For example, Bob sells Sally a car, which she drives, and pollutes the air the rest of us breathe in. We never agreed to this and are therefore suffering an externality, which we need a government to solve. The problem is that the existence of a state is itself an externality. A few people in Parliament or Congress write and impose laws upon millions of people, forcing them to do things that they may not have agreed to do voluntarily. Historically, when governments have enslaved people as military conscripts and murdered people in war, they never did care to obtain the consent of those getting murdered or enslaved to do such things.

Short-Sightedness: Seldom are long-term consequences considered when politicians and voters are considering passing legislation. Do politicians ever go to jail for breach of contract when they campaign on policy X and never follow through on passing policy X? How often do politicians go to jail for war crimes? Take an American example. Progressive President Woodrow Wilson gained a lot of power and influence by implementing the federal income tax, the Federal Reserve System, and declaring war on Germany, but he never faced any fines or jail time for such disastrous policies. Lyndon Johnson started a "War on Poverty" which never ended poverty, nor drastically decreased it. Richard Nixon claimed in August 1971 that the U.S. would "temporarily" leave the gold standard, but the U.S. has yet to return to having a gold-backed currency, and Nixon was never held accountable. On August 29, 2021, President Joseph Biden killed seven children and three adult civilians in Afghanistan and has yet to be put in jail. Members of the police and military are short-sighted in so far as they take an oath to enforce immoral laws, which have harmed people for decades, in exchange for a paycheck in the present.

Greed: Somehow, a system of mutually beneficial, voluntary exchanges has earned the "greedy" badge, while politics, the system of forcing people to fund or do things that they vehemently oppose, has earned the badge of "society."

A central claim of Progressivism is the appeal to "public goods." As defined by the Corporate Finance Institute, public goods are "commonly available to all people within a society or community" and "possess two specific qualities: they are *non-excludable* and *non-rivalrous*. Everyone has access to use them, and their use does not deplete their availability for future use" (emphasis mine).[28] Common examples include governments providing police and military services – everyone is said to benefit if the community is kept safe, therefore it is a public good and people must be forced to fund it by law.

Again, notice how the existence of "public goods" does not automatically justify ushering in a monopoly on violence (a state), since the state too is subject to the problem of public goods – i.e., people reaping benefits from others who had to bear the cost of producing. Even today, not everyone is a net taxpayer, which means that some people are benefitting at the cost of others.

Compare the percentage of people involved in the process of passing laws to the percentage of people who benefit from or bear the costs of those laws. For the sake of argument, assume you support school choice, i.e., the concept that any citizen can send his child to any public school, not just the one they happen to live closest to. You will spend untold hours at meetings, countless more hours reading research on the topic, and plenty of your own money to set up campaign rallies to make persuasive arguments to your fellow citizens while donating to certain political candidates in the process. If the school choice law you have championed passes, millions will benefit at your expense because of the uncompensated work you performed.

In 2014, Americans like John J. Mearsheimer spent time and reputational risk coming out against a coup taking place in Ukraine against the government of Viktor Yanukovych, claiming the United States was using NGOs (Non-Governmental Organizations) such as the National Endowment for Democracy to provoke a potential Third World War with Russia by installing a hostile regime on Russia's border. International relations theorists such as Mearsheimer have had to bear the cost, and today we benefit from their wisdom more than ever.

To be clear, there is nothing wrong with people choosing to work hard to better the lives of others; the central issue is the claim that having a government solves the issue of public goods.

As Dr. Christopher Freiman puts it in his book *Unequivocal Justice: Political Philosophy for the Real World*: "Free riders won't pay the costs of good government for the same reason why they won't pay the costs of clean air: they don't have to. They'll profit from the good votes of others even if they vote badly or not at all."[29]

Another way to falsify the thesis that "government is necessary for people to reap benefits for things they do not pay for" can be to see whether the voluntary sector of society has provided such goods.

Here are two noteworthy examples of beautiful, privately funded artistic structures. The first is in England:

> 765 years ago, the Salisbury Cathedral was consecrated in England. Considered the oldest example of early Gothic architecture in England, the old beauty maintains the largest cloister, the tallest spire, and the largest external park or "cathedral close," of any cathedral in Britain. Inside are also one of the oldest continual-working clocks, and one of the 4 surviving copies of the Magna Carta.
>
> Construction was paid for by donations, principally from the canons and vicars of southeast England, who were asked to contribute a fixed annual sum until the building was completed.[30]

The second is in America:

> The Statue of Liberty's creators believed the project should be a joint effort. The French would pay for the statue; the people of the United States would fund the pedestal. The Franco-American Union was established in 1875 by Édouard René Lefèbvre de Laboulaye to oversee the project. The French Committee, established the same year, was created to coordinate the fundraising in France and the American Committee, established in 1877, was to coordinate fundraising in the United States.
>
> Fundraising included advertising, exhibitions, public events, and the sale of souvenirs. Though wealthy individuals did contribute, it was the small donations of hundreds of thousands of working people and children on both sides of the Atlantic that made the Statue of Liberty a reality.[31]

Non-Profit Source reports that in 2020 Americans alone gave $471.44 billion to charities. Platforms such as GoFundMe, IndieGoGo, Amazon Smile, and Kickstarter have facilitated the giving of billions more to people in need through the voluntary sector.

When facing any issue in society, it's important to ask which group of people have the knowledge to improve the situation and the incentive to make such changes arise. The most well-meaning people in society cannot "solve" poverty or ignorance if they themselves do not understand why some people and nations are wealthy and others are not.

Even if one does claim to have the knowledge necessary, say, to "bring democracy to Libya," does he have an incentive to make sure that such a thing is done without massive long-term harm to civilians? Politicians and voters almost are never punished for supporting bad policies, no matter how disastrous, and thus their incentive to avoid them is negligible.

A Cleansing Process

A free-market system is superior morally and economically to Progressivism because it allows people voluntarily to opt out of funding or participating with bad actors, without the threat of going to jail. While the process is far from perfect, it is far superior to one that does not allow for such peaceful disassociation.

5. College: Four Years of Work for $0.00 an Hour

> It is utterly embarrassing that "pay people enough to live" is a stance
> that's even up for debate. Override the parliamentarian and raise the
> wage.
>
> – Congresswoman Alexandria Ocasio-Cortez[32]

I remember debating the minimum wage while attending Arizona State
University, and in the midst of the debate it occurred to me that I had spent
thousands and thousands of hours of my life working on in-class
assignments and homework.

No one ever paid me a dime for all this labor.

If the Progressive principle is that "everyone who works for one hour
should earn $15 per hour," they must admit that what students do in college
for zero pay is work — making it far more "exploitative" than even a job
that pays $1 an hour, where at least the person gets on-the-job experience.

Knowing that higher costs disproportionately hurt small business, it's no
surprise that both former and current Walmart CEOs (H. Lee Scott[33] and
Doug McMillon[34]) have come out in favor of raising the minimum wage.

The Progressive will readily concede that higher healthcare costs decrease
the likelihood that the poor will be able to access healthcare. In the same
breath, he will refuse to admit that raising the cost of employment decreases
the likelihood that businesses will hire employees, especially those who are
inexperienced and possess few marketable skills.

While the intention of helping those struggling appears to be admirable,
the lack of concern the Progressive has for why wages rise renders this
intention shallow. Little if any attention from Progressive news outlets is ever
dedicated to urging people to gain skills that will allow them to demand a
higher wage in the workplace.

The *goal* vs. *process* distinction is often ignored. Most everyone has a *goal*
to see people with greater access to higher wages, nice houses, and education.
The question is which *process* or set of rules should be embraced to increase
the likelihood of such an outcome. The clear answer is a *process* which
embraces the freedom and choices of individuals to cooperate voluntarily,

which increases the likelihood of their making mutually beneficial economic exchanges.

Wages and working conditions improve as a result of capital investment and competition amongst employers. When I worked at Walmart, our handheld computer system went down for one day, and we had to fill out orders with pen and paper. If memory serves, we served one-tenth of the customers that day. Without all the capital infrastructure, which costs employers millions of dollars, we were only about 10 percent as productive as we otherwise would have been, making our labor worth less to employers.

As Milton and Rose Friedman explain in their book *Free to Choose*[35]:

> The most reliable and effective protection for most workers is provided by the existence of many employers. As we have seen, a person who has only one possible employer has little or no protection. The employers who protect a worker are those who would like to hire him. Their demand for his services makes it in the self-interest of his own employer to pay him the full value of his work. If his own employer doesn't, someone else may be ready to do so. Competition for his services — that is the worker's real protection.

Competition among employers to improve employee treatment explains why only 1.4 percent of all hourly paid workers earn the federal minimum wage.[36] It also explains the drastic decrease in workplace deaths[37] that occurred decades before the federal government created the Occupational Safety and Health Administration (OSHA):

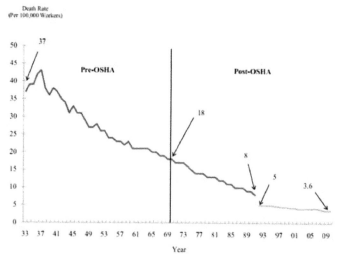

FIGURE 1: WORKPLACE FATALITIES, 1933–2010

Sources: National Safety Council (1994) and US Department of Labor, Bureau of Labor Statistics (2012)

Democratic Socialism, a subset of Progressivism, also advocates the Labor Theory of (Surplus) Value, claiming that the value of a good or service is derived from the amount of labor it took to make it; thus, "employers" are parasites stealing the value of the workers.

This would mean that all welfare recipients are stealing our surplus value. Even volunteer work (no pay for labor) violates this principle. Volunteer work that pays $0.00 an hour would necessarily be abolished if the minimum wage principle were to be accepted. Pensions would also have to be abolished, since the person receiving the money is no longer working — only in a free market system could such voluntary contracts be entertained.

This assumes that no value is brought to the table by investors — those who come up with the idea of what to sell, where to sell it, how to market it to consumers, how to train employees, where to source wholesale products — and it rejects the workers' right to contract voluntarily.

Progressives will often claim that the need for people to attend university lies in the importance of an educated populace. Seldom do they realize that this is an implicit admission that thirteen years of kindergarten through high school government schooling has not yielded impressive results.

The Progressive push for more people getting into university has also caused credential inflation, defined by SociologyDictionary.com as "the tendency to require ever-increasing, often unnecessary, levels of education or qualifications (e.g., certificates, degrees, and diplomas) for a specific job."

With more students in classes, teachers lower their standards, students on average learn less, and the next generation of workers and consumers at all levels of society have less access to quality goods and services. Learning on the job teaches people far more important skills, such as how to interact with customers and create value for value exchanges.

A "politically informed population" is also a fool's errand. You cannot reasonably expect people to sacrifice all the time necessary to evaluate candidates; read past legislation, judicial rulings, and pending legislation; watch debates; and research the track records of politicians. Not to mention, you'd like them to have a general understanding of history, economics, political science, energy policy, agricultural policy, foreign policy, statistics, and philosophy, as well as the ability to see through propaganda.

And once they spend all that scarce time and money, they get a one-in-a-few-million vote between two candidates (both of whom are probably ignorant themselves on these issues).

19

The assumption that poor people couldn't freely access schooling or education is unjustifiable. There are many churches around the world where people donate to raise funds and allow everyone to attend. In these churches, there are a variety of choices (not one monopoly as Progressivism would predict), and almost everyone can go to church for free.

Studies show (to use a favorite expression of the Progressive) that this is an empirical reality not just for "the rich" but also for the Third World. In 2012, Pauline Dixon published her findings at *Econ Journal Watch* in a study titled "Why the Denial? Low-Cost Private Schools in Developing Countries and Their Contributions to Education," a follow-up to her previous study with James Tooly at the Cato Institute titled "Private Education Is Good for the Poor: A Study of Private Schools Serving the Poor in Low-Income Countries."[38] Focusing mostly on countries in Asia and Africa, the second paper summarizes its major findings as follows:

- The majority of poor parents choose private unaided schools for their children.

- Teacher costs are significantly less in private unaided schools than in government schools.

- Gender equity is maintained in private unaided school enrollment.

- School enrollment is underestimated.

- Free primary education serves to crowd out private schools and does not increase overall enrollment.

- Better pupil-teacher ratios prevail in private unaided than in government schools.

- More teaching is occurring in private than in government schools.

- The poorest children are given free or subsidized seats in private schools.

- Rather than assume that the private unaided education sector is a problem, we should see it as a great strength.

Other examples of sources of free education include Wikipedia, Khan Academy, YouTube.com, Odysse.com, LibertarianInstitute.org, and the *Don't Tread on Anyone* podcast.

Even in the education sector, freedom of contracts creates more choices and provides an incentive for higher quality at a lower cost.

The Progressive cannot consistently defend things such as volunteer work, college, or private schooling. Only the free market advocate who says that all economic activity between consenting adults must be decriminalized can do so, making this another reason I left Progressivism.

6. Equality and the Iron Law of Oligarchy

All complex organizations, regardless of how democratic they are when started, eventually develop into oligarchies....Since no sufficiently large and complex organization can function purely as a direct democracy, power within an organization will always get delegated to individuals within that group, elected or otherwise.

– Iron Law of Oligarchy[39]

Progressives have long claimed that a desire for equality is their North Star when it comes to which policies should be enacted.

Equality (of power, opportunity, outcome, or influence) is another fool's errand which cannot be achieved in any society.

The classic example is that of a labor union.

Not every worker attends the meetings. Not everyone who attends speaks at the meetings. Not everyone who speaks has good ideas. Not everyone who has good ideas is courageous enough to speak up and risk being dismissed. Not everyone has equal communication skills to persuade the union as to why they should vote for this or that. So you end up with very few union members having a disproportionately large influence and the vast majority having no influence.

Even in the narrowest circumstances, people act and engage in a division of labor based on talents which are always wide-ranging.

A small percentage of comedians become popular. A small percentage of bands sell out stadiums. A small percentage of professional athletes get most of the media attention and sell most of the jerseys. A small percentage of authors dominate bookshelves. A small percentage of movie directors get the vast majority of film viewership. A small percentage of YouTube content creators have more than a billion views, while most struggle to break 10,000.

The moment humans act, they pursue goals which some people are better at achieving than others. This instantly creates inequality.

This also applies to the political realm, which Progressives believe will eradicate such inequality.

A small percentage of politicians dominate the news, pass legislation, and alter public opinion.

How many Chinese people were equal in power to Chairman Mao? How many Russian citizens were equal in power to Joseph Stalin? How many Prussians were equal in power to Otto von Bismarck? Today, what percentage of citizens are as equally as powerful as America's Joseph Biden? North Korea's Kim Jong Un? Ukraine's Volodymyr Zelenskyy? Russia's Vladimir Putin? China's Xi Jinping?

Historically, the same applies for Aristotle, Mansa Musa, Genghis Khan, Cleopatra, Henry Ford, Martin Luther King, Jr., The Beatles, Albert Einstein, Queen Elizabeth I, Meryl Streep, Michael Jordan, and Marshall Mathers. In every case, there exists a lot of power and influence concentrated in the hands of a few in every aspect of every society since the beginning of time.

Even Progressives such as Jeremy Corbyn, Nicolás Maduro, Bernie Sanders, Ilhan Omar, and Alexandria Ocasio-Cortez have more institutional power than 99.99% of their supporters ever will.

As many have noted before, the very reason why some of the most powerful people in society promote the unachievable idea of equality is precisely that it is unachievable. Once the population has been led to believe that inequality of outcome is inherently bad and that one day equality can be achieved, the state can justify its control over all aspects of society indefinitely.

Once we recognize inequality as the norm, we need to ask: "Which system or social arrangement limits potential harm by the inevitable oligarchy, while making it work in the general interests of the masses?"

The answer is a system which allows people to associate and disassociate freely with their time and money — which automatically rules out Progressivism and any form of state apparatus.

Numerous economists have compared the inequality provided by the state (courts, schools, central banks, policing) to the inequality in more privatized industries (food, electronics, clothing, transit) as evidence that if you are in favor of equality, the best system to support is one in which businesses have an incentive to produce and compete for the consumer's voluntarily given dollar.

Progressives have taken something that exists everywhere and always — inequality — and pinned it uniquely on the free market.

Is there any relationship more unequal than that of the citizen to the state?

As discussed previously, the state claims exclusive rights to do things to citizens (tax, regulate, conscript, declare war, etc.) that no other organization can rightfully do.

A final plea to equality can be made on the grounds that "why should the rich like Elon Musk get space flights while others starve?"

We are fortunate that these people weren't calling the shots in the past in so many sectors of the economy. We can safely assume that the Progressive would have said, "The Wright Brothers need to stop playing air-games and have their wealth from their bike shop confiscated and redistributed."

It takes a vast amount of time, research, development, money, and trial-and-error to bring a product from stage one (idea) to the consumer. Planes, computers, televisions, cell phones, book distribution, and printing methods all required massive amounts of investment, which was paid for by a small few who could afford to purchase early versions of the product. These "early adopters" paid high costs, and over time, the prices of these goods and services got lower and their quality increased, allowing the masses eventually to access them.

The Santa Claus mindset — that things just exist out of nowhere and everyone has access to them — is central to the economic illiteracy of Progressivism.

The "wealthy" statistics often floated around do not distinguish between the amount of money a person has on hand and his overall net worth. While a business owner might be worth $20 billion, that simply means that he has a network of contracts, investments, and property values which cumulatively are estimated to be worth $20 billion. It does not mean that the person has a bank account with $20 billion in cash available at any time. If Progressives had their dream of confiscating all wealth from all American billionaires, it would not even fund the federal government for a single year.[40]

The vilification of "the rich" also does not distinguish between people who are wealthy as a result of meeting consumer demand voluntarily and those who have acquired wealth through fraud or violence. Lyft, Zoom, Apple, Kroger, YouTube, Ikea, Google Drive, Walmart, Netflix, and Amazon offer poor people more access to products and services than any Progressive regime could have imagined.

Rich vs. poor is another false divide — like claiming that the average American is the enemy of the average Haitian because they are vastly unequal in terms of wealth — which is another reason I abandoned Progressivism.

7. Voter Suppression vs. Economic Suppression

In a world where some people have so much, any person capable of empathy is heartbroken at the sight of someone who is without a home.

The important fallacy to avoid when discussing such emotional topics is: Bad thing X exists; therefore, the government has the knowledge, ability, and incentives to solve X, and people should be forced to fund it via taxation and be jailed if they don't chip in.

Here are three real-world examples of how Progressive regulatory policies harm the very vulnerable people they claim to fight for:

> At a cost that ranges from $10,000 to $50,000, tiny homes like the Matchbox could help to ease the shortage of affordable housing in the capital city. Heating and cooling costs are negligible. Rainwater catchment systems help to make the homes self-sustaining. They're an attractive option to the very sort of residents who the city attracts in abundance: single, young professionals without a lot of stuff, who aren't ready to take on a large mortgage.

> But tiny houses come with one enormous catch: they're illegal, in violation of several codes in Washington, D.C.'s Zoning Ordinance. Among the many requirements in the 34 chapters and 600 pages of code are mandates defining minimum lot size, room sizes, alleyway widths, and "accessory dwelling units" that prevent tiny houses from being anything more than a part-time residence.[41]

> – Todd Krainin, "Jay Austin's Beautiful, Illegal Tiny House," *Reason*, August 9, 2014.

> Elvis Summers crowdfunded $100,000 and built dozens of $1,200 tiny houses for the homeless. Then the city seized them...

> Each night, tens of thousands of people sleep in tent cities crowding the palm-lined boulevards of Los Angeles, far more than any other city in the nation. The homeless population in the entertainment capital of the world has hit new record highs in each of the past few years.

> But a 39-year-old struggling musician from South L.A. thought he had a creative fix. Elvis Summers, who went through stretches of homelessness himself in his 20s, raised over $100,000 through crowdfunding campaigns last spring. With the help of professional contractors and others in the community who sign up to volunteer

through his nonprofit, Starting Human, he has built dozens of solar-powered, tiny houses to shelter the homeless since.

Summers says that the houses are meant to be a temporary solution that, unlike a tent, provides the secure foundation residents need to improve their lives. "The tiny houses provide immediate shelter," he explains. "People can lock their stuff up and know that when they come back from their drug treatment program or court or finding a job all day, their stuff is where they left it."

Each house features a solar power system, a steel-reinforced door, a camping toilet, a smoke detector, and even window alarms. The tiny structures cost Summers roughly $1,200 apiece to build.

L.A. city officials, however, had a different plan to address the crisis. A decade after the city's first 10-year plan to end homelessness withered in 2006, Mayor Eric Garcetti announced in February a $1.87 billion proposal to get all L.A. residents off the streets, once and for all. He and the City Council aim to build 10,000 units of permanent housing with supportive services over the next decade. In the interim, they are shifting funds away from temporary and emergency shelters.

Councilmember Curren Price, who represents the district where Summers's tiny houses were located, does not believe they are beneficial either to the community or to the homeless people housed in them. "I don't really want to call them houses. They're really just boxes," says Price. "They're not safe, and they impose real hazards for neighbors in the community."

Most of Summers's tiny houses are on private land that has been donated to the project. A handful had replaced the tents that have proliferated on freeway overpasses in the city. Summers put them there until he could secure a private lot to create a tiny house village similar to those that already exist in Portland, Seattle, Austin, and elsewhere. "My whole issue and cause is that something needs to be done right now," Summers emphasizes. But the houses, nestled among dour tent shantytowns, became brightly colored targets early this year for frustrated residents who want the homeless out of their backyards. Councilmember Price was bombarded by complaints from angry constituents.

In February, the City Council responded by amending a sweeps ordinance to allow the tiny houses to be seized without prior notice. On the morning of the ninth, just as the mayor and council gathered at City Hall to announce their new plan to end homelessness, police and garbage trucks descended on the tiny homes, towing three of them to a Bureau of Sanitation lot for disposal. Summers managed to move eight of the threatened houses into storage before they were confiscated, but their residents were left back on the sidewalk.[42]

– Justin Monticello, "This L.A. Musician Built $1,200 Tiny Houses for the Homeless," *Reason*, December 9, 2016.

KANSAS CITY, Mo. — The Health Department is speaking out after it poured bleach on food intended to be given to the homeless.

Nellie McCool, who helps run "Free Hot Soup Kansas City," has been helping the homeless for years until Sunday.

"Officers and health inspectors demanded we destroy our food and we were violating health code violations by sharing meals with our friends," said McCool.

The department said the group wasn't following the law about serving the homeless.

"They were notified back in a meeting in September that they needed to get a permit and they just outright said they refused to do that," said Dr. Rex Archer, Director of Health for KCMO.

"At one of the sites, where they were informed that they were not going to be able to serve because they didn't have a permit and weren't doing it safely, they actually threw some of the food at our inspector," said Archer.

McCool disputes that claiming someone in the group got upset and threw the food on the ground. Inspectors then poured bleach on the food to make sure no one ate it.

"Standard procedure in public health is to go ahead and pour bleach on the food. So, that people won't consume something that is dangerous," said Dr. Archer.[43]

– Jordan Betts, "Health Dept. Defends Bleaching Food for Homeless," KSHB 41 Kansas City News, November 5, 2018.

Many political discussions can become philosophical abstractions or debates about the minutiae of this or that future implication of a piece of legislation.

We often forget that real human lives are at stake when Progressives advocate using state coercion to "keep us safe."

The lesson: The most vulnerable people in society were being voluntarily helped, but then the state coercively intervened under the guise of keeping them safe, only to make them worse off.

It's very common for people to become the very things they set out to oppose. Progressives clearly see this when conservatives claim passionately to oppose terrorism, while condoning their own government's murder of civilians to achieve such an end.

When it comes to caring about those in poverty, Progressives will assume that hating the "rich" necessarily means that they care about the "poor."

Progressives will encourage us to vote, since voting reflects our desires (even though your one vote does not change the overall outcome), but then, for our own good, not allow us to live voluntarily in the house of our own choosing. This is no different in principle from the imperialism and colonialism the Progressive claims to oppose.

The ignorance lies first in not recognizing that people often choose bad things because it's their best alternative. The Progressive mindset does not ask: "Compared to what?"

Yes, someone may be working for a low wage or living in poor conditions, or eating low-quality food. The Progressive response to this is to legislate the job, house, and food out of existence, leaving the poor person with nothing at all.

Progressives will vilify those who voluntarily offer us jobs, products, and services before ever having a peaceful alternative. They assume that good things happen automatically; therefore, if something bad exists, it's because some bad actor created the situation. This is most often seen when someone discusses the causes of poverty, not appreciating that poverty is the natural state of mankind and the important question is: "What causes wealth?"

Yes, small houses are bad compared to big houses. But when someone's choices are between homelessness and a small house, the state has no right to confiscate the house.

All the billions of leftists on earth have every right to start a GoFundMe (or any form of voluntary fundraising) to offer better alternatives to those in vulnerable positions. They don't have the right to criminalize voluntary economic activities between consenting adults.

The most common real-world justification for commercial regulation in the modern day is the "Repeal of Glass-Steagall Act" that took place in the 1990s. History.com summarizes the original Glass-Steagall Act as "part of the Banking Act of 1933, [a] landmark banking legislation that separated Wall Street from Main Street by offering protection to people who entrust their savings to commercial banks."

The claim: Through deregulation, banks became able to take massive amounts of risks which led to an overly volatile market causing the recession of 2007–08.

The reality: This theory can be judged by looking at which banks in 2007 were most volatile (who went bankrupt) and see whether they were banks which only took such risks as a causal result of the Glass-Steagall repeal. The main firms involved in the 2007–08 crash were investment firms Lehman Brothers and Bear Stearns, and insurance firm American International Group. It turns out the most volatile would have taken the same type of risks, as any economist would assume that whatever banks couldn't diversify would be less stable — the exact opposite of the Glass-Steagall myth.

Homelessness is one of the many examples of how the Progressive policies are initially sold to the masses by creating a rich boogeyman, and then, when the very same justification for regulation is used to strip people from their houses, we get no retractions, nor any apologies from the people who created this situation.

"My Body, My Choice," the Progressive so often proudly claims. The problem is, this principle advocated consistently must lead one to reject the concept of government permits or licensing, since licensing necessarily involves criminalizing economic activity between consenting adults.

The false dichotomy is: "We either have standards, or have no standards." The reality is that we either have monopoly standards or competing standards. Today, certification (think "stamp of approval") agencies are all around us, such as Underwriters Laboratories, Bureau Veritas, Consumer Reports, Amazon Customer Reviews, Good Housekeeping Seal, and Yelp. Each person in a free-market economy is himself a regulator in so far as with whom he chooses to do business.

Even when it comes to the security of persons and their property, we see consumer demand for such security being met with market opportunities. While security is frequently assumed to be something that only a government can provide, organizations such as Sentinel-1 and Webroot provide computer security, where most of our valuable data is stored. Organizations like PayPal and Venmo have private security centers to keep people's money safe. Banks, sports stadiums, night clubs, shopping malls, and business centers also find it in their best interest to provide customers a secure environment. Far from the free market being a constant war of all against all, businesses are constantly regulating their operations on a voluntary basis.

A common justification for government "regulation" (a euphemism for violently stopping consenting adults from engaging in peaceful exchanges) is: "I am not only a Progressive, but also a realist, and I just don't trust people to do the right thing on their own."

First, this does not account for a customer's right or ability to stop doing business with a person or group. The customer's ability to disassociate from bad actors is the ultimate regulation (or check and balance) in a civilized society.

Second, it's worth noting that politicians and government officials are members of the fallible human race as well.

If people "can't be trusted," then we can't have a state police with the right to arrest people for victimless crimes. We can't have a state military, since they could just invade countries for personal gain. We can't have government schools, since teachers and administrators cannot be trusted. We can't have welfare, since welfare recipients could cheat the system. We can't have government judges, since people cannot be trusted. We can't have politicians, since they'll act in a greedy manner; nor can we allow people to vote, since, after all, people cannot be trusted.

Notice how every criticism of the free-market society applies many times over to a society with a state. Yet even this does not mean that both are equally fallible, since a state does not allow people to disassociate from bad actors. It mandates taxation, conscription, and regulation with no consideration of the consent, or lack thereof, of the parties involved.

The question — in cases of, say, military conscription — is not whether we should defend ourselves. The question is who gets to decide what is worth defending, and to what extent. Either the people themselves decide, or politicians unilaterally designate themselves as surrogate decision makers.

There is a common trend where people will analyze historical incidents based on objective principles, and the present in matters of utility (benefits to persons). People correctly say slavery was evil, the German National Socialist Workers Party was evil, Jim Crow laws were evil, the Rape of Nanjing was evil, Native American massacres were evil, etc.

Yet in the present, especially when it comes to something like pouring bleach on food instead of giving it to the most vulnerable people in society, it is often shrugged off: "Well, that's the law we have to follow. If you don't like it, work to change it." Or, more commonly: "Well, studies show..." Imagine saying, "I don't love the idea of slavery, but freeing millions of ignorant people to roam around as they please would be chaotic, and before I oppose Jim Crow laws, I must see numerous expert-driven, long-term studies that indicate how desegregation will be beneficial to society at large."

This type of utilitarian approach leaves a gaping hole for tyrants to use the government, media, and education system to cherry-pick portions of reality to fit the narrative they wish to promote, which will inevitably lead to more unjust power for themselves.

By not respecting the right of all adult persons to engage in mutually beneficial voluntary exchanges, Progressivism comes into direct conflict with the "My Body, My Choice" principle it claims to champion.

Imagine two criminals:

Criminal 1: Forcibly stops a woman from having a one-in-10-million vote to determine the governor of her state.

Criminal 2: Forcibly stops a woman from getting the job of her dreams as a hair stylist via occupational licensing regulations, even though a willing employer wanted to hire her and customers wanted her service.

You are the judge in both trials: Which criminal should get a longer sentence?

Criminal 1's actions may be offensive, but have no effect on the outcome of the woman's life, since a one-in-10-million vote will make no difference in the outcome of an election. Even if by some miracle she happened to be the deciding vote, politicians are commonly understood to be liars, and whomever she elected would likely keep all of his bad promises and follow through on none of the good ones.*[44]

Criminal 2, however, has forcibly stopped her from directly experiencing the life she wants to live. Eight hours a day, five days a week, she is worse off because a Progressive Imperialist is criminalizing a capitalist act between consenting adults. She now is also deprived of getting on-the-job experience and a foot in the door into an industry which she is passionate about.

The Cato Institute has reported that, far from being a small issue, "[t]he share of U.S. jobs requiring an occupational license increased from 5% in the 1950s to 22% in 2021."[45]

This is Progressive Imperialism. If your neighbor has forcibly stopped you from doing something peaceful, it doesn't matter whether a vote was

---

* Horton's Law: "Politicians can be counted on to keep all their bad promises and abandon all their good ones."

first taken, or whether this order came from someone 12,000 miles away. It's imperialism nonetheless.

The Progressive Imperialist not only deprives millions of poor people of job opportunities, but also advocates that their purchasing power be severely limited by regulations. You want to buy a product or service with the money you rightfully earned? Too bad. Democratic Imperialists haven't given it their stamp of approval.

Progressives claim that needing a single driver's license can stop large numbers of poor people from being able to vote. The assumption is that the poor do not have the monetary resources, necessary knowledge, or time to go to the DMV to get a license to prove their identity. Thus, the poor would not be able to vote if such identification were mandatory to show at voting polls, and the poor would not be democratically represented.

"What we learned in this election and what we saw every day with our eyes is the incredible degree of voter suppression which exists out there," said Senator Bernie Sanders in November 2020.[46]

According to Progressivism, requiring a single license in order to vote harms the poor, whereas requiring dozens of licenses and decades of training in order to work in the marketplace helps the poor.

Progressives cannot consistently claim to support the poor while also advocating that they be jailed for participating in capitalist acts between consenting adults.

8. Government-Provided
Does Not Mean "Universal"

The following is written in response to Steven Grumbine, the founder of Real Progressives, after he claimed that libertarians were murder advocates for supporting a reduction in the size of government, also known as "austerity."

What is wrong with the following logic? "Steven Grumbine advocates decreasing military spending (also known as military austerity). Therefore, Grumbine wants America to get invaded, enslaved, and suffer a genocide."

Wanting to decrease expenditure on military does not imply that you don't care about defense. The unjustifiable assumption is that more military spending means Americans are automatically safer as a causal result of increased spending. As Mr. Grumbine and I agree, increased military spending leads to unnecessary invasions, which create blowback and enemies, which make the United States less safe.

Now what's wrong with this one? Let's say that Steven Grumbine opposes Costco's right to take 20 percent of everyone's income by force and give us "free and universal" Costco schooling for thirteen years in exchange. Therefore, Steven Grumbine wants everyone to be stupid and doesn't care whether some people get an education and a happy life while others die via ignorance.

Grumbine denies that Costco has the right to do this.

The problem with this logic is that it could easily be the case that Mr. Grumbine cares deeply about education, but he just doesn't believe that Costco is a suitable organization to achieve such an end. He also could believe that, even if Costco is a great organization, people shouldn't be forced to fund it and get caged if they don't chip in.

The reason why this matters is that Mr. Grumbine has accused libertarians of advocating economic "austerity" and thus advocating murder.

Apparently, Mr. Grumbine sees the Federal government spending $6.27 trillion[47] in 2022 and says, "Anyone who doesn't want them to get even more money wants people to die."

Giving the state more power to produce healthcare has not lowered the price of healthcare. Giving the state billions to provide schools hasn't given every high school graduate an educated mind, even with an increase of 280 percent (adjusted for inflation) in per-student spending since 1960.[48] Fannie & Freddie government-backed home loans didn't cure homelessness. The Federal Reserve's monopolization of the money supply has neither stopped recessions nor kept inflation from occurring. The court system does not create "universal justice," nor do government police create "universal safety." Sallie Mae and college subsidies have not increased the quality of schooling, nor have they decreased the cost. The "War on Drugs" has not helped drug addicts or their families, and invading Afghanistan didn't usher in peace and prosperity for Afghans.

In short, opposing government intervention in X in no way means that people don't care about X.

Facebook, Southwest Airlines, Uber, Goodwill, Twitter, Skype, and Google Maps all provide quality products to poor people at low or no cost.

In *Race and Economics*, economist Walter E. Williams explains:

> Consider another comparison between market- and political-resource allocation. If one tours a low-income black neighborhood, he will see people wearing some nice clothing, eating some nice food, driving some nice cars, and he might even see some nice houses — but no nice schools. Why? The answer relates directly to how clothing, food, cars, and houses — versus schools — are allocated. Clothing, food, cars, and houses are allocated through the market mechanism. Schools, for the most part, are parceled out through the political mechanism. *If a buyer is dissatisfied with goods distributed in the market, the individual can simply "fire" the producer by taking his business elsewhere. If a buyer (taxpayer) is dissatisfied with a public school, such an option is not, in a black neighborhood, economically available to him.* He has to bear the burden of moving to a neighborhood with better schools. Interestingly, if one does see high quality schools in poor or moderate-income black neighborhoods, they tend to be private institutions, such as Ivy Leaf in Philadelphia, Marcus Garvey in Los Angeles, and Marva Collins Prep in Chicago.[49] (emphasis mine)

Progressives support what is called "universal healthcare." The term "universal" implies that there are two options — either everyone can have healthcare, or some must go without.

This assumes that giving the government a coercively funded monopoly on providing a service will render it in a state of universal abundance.

The government in America gives us "universal" schooling. Does that mean that everyone is smart? Government provides judicial courts. Does that mean that everyone gets universally guaranteed justice? Government provides police. Does this yield universal, quality protection? Government provides the military. Does this give everyone universal safety?

In September 2015, a CNN headline read as follows: "307,000 veterans may have died awaiting Veterans Affairs health care, report says." Government control in no way leads to "universality."

The Progressive almost always leaves out the fact that the U.S. government already plays a major role in the healthcare industry with Medicare, Medicaid, the Food and Drug Administration, occupational licensing, and the Affordable Care Act.

According to Progressive columnist Paul Krugman: "In 2004 government programs paid for 44 percent of healthcare in America, while private insurance paid for only 36 percent."[50]

Krugman goes on to concede that the American insurance system he now loathes was the result of Progressive policies, saying:

> [T]he great majority of Americans who do have private health insurance get it through their employers. This is partly the result of history — during World War II companies weren't allowed to raise wages to compete for workers, so many offered health benefits instead.

The claim that "we Progressives want everyone to have X, so if you disagree with our approach, you must want people to go without X" gives Progressives such radical confidence in their position. Refuting this false concept is vitally important.

If we compare the most subsidized and regulated sectors of the economy with the least subsidized and regulated, a clear pattern emerges.

More regulations result in higher entry and operational costs, leading to fewer competitors in a given industry, fewer choices for consumers, and fewer employment opportunities for workers.

When the state subsidizes an industry, producers focus on pleasing politicians and ignore consumers; hence, the rising costs of housing, healthcare, and schooling — the three industries that the government has subsidized the most (besides the military, which is also not known for cost efficiency). Compare this to much more privately produced goods (such as TVs, phones, computers, software, toys, clothing, and furniture) which have increased in quality and decreased in price[51]:

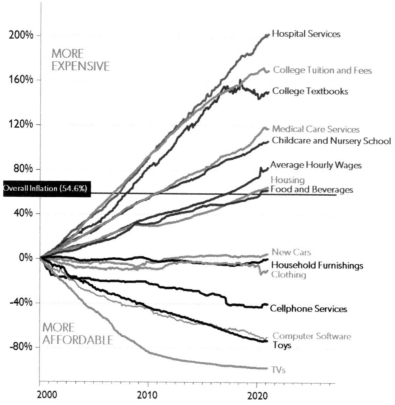

Price Changes: January 2000 to December 2020
Selected US Consumer Goods and Services, Wages

The other Progressive approach to related issues is to say, "Service X should be free." What they are actually advocating is that the government pay for it after it has taken a large percentage of people's income by force.

If you said to the average Progressive, "Stop complaining about military spending. The military is free since the government pays for it," the Progressive would rightfully laugh. However, when it comes to Progressives' pet projects, the word *free* is used without hesitation. To have free schooling, for example, would entail that teachers all be unpaid volunteers, that the construction workers who built the school be unpaid, that the custodians be unpaid, etc. To imply that it's free once you pay taxes is tantamount to saying, "Ruth's Chris Steak House is free. You just pay afterwards."

Everything is "free," once you pay for it. In this case, it's "free" once the state forcibly confiscates at least 30 percent of your annual income.

Even in a moneyless society, every resource — including time, cement, light bulbs, or real estate — is still scarce, and you therefore bear an opportunity cost when using resources to achieve X instead of Y. The Progressive might see things more clearly if we said, "Everyone should be forced to pay for the Koch Brothers Business Education; then, everyone could access it free of charge." Such a proposal is clearly just one group of people trying to get their ideas promoted and subsidized at the expense of everyone else.

Another method of measuring how the poor become wealthier is to look at a single industry and then to compare the most government-regulated aspects of that industry to the least regulated aspects of that industry.

To get an overall idea of how much the economy is burdened with economic sanctions, George Washington University has gathered research on the "Total Number of Pages Published in the Code of Federal Regulations (1950-2021)":

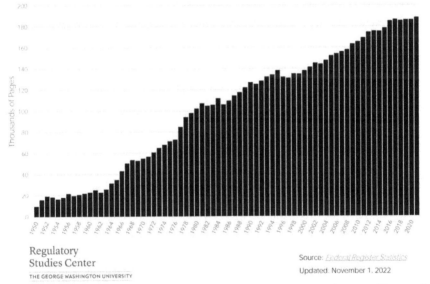

Regulatory
Studies Center
THE GEORGE WASHINGTON UNIVERSITY

Source: *Federal Register Statistics*
Updated: November 1, 2022

In the education sector, places like InternetArchive.org have millions of free books for immediate viewing or download. According to Wikipedia (another free educational resource): "The Internet Archive is an American digital library founded on May 10, 1996, and chaired by free information advocate Brewster Kahle. It provides free access to collections of digitized materials like websites, software applications, music, audiovisual and print materials."

Amazon has drastically increased the number of books available to the average person, while providing more low-cost alternatives, resulting in more people having access to a low-cost education than ever before — if they want it.

While we also see a significant increase in healthcare costs in recent times, it's worth noting how much the quality has increased.

The case of Calvin Coolidge (U.S. President, 1923–29) is illustrative. According to the Coolidge Foundation:

> [W]hile playing lawn tennis with his brother on the White House grounds, sixteen-year-old Calvin, Jr., developed a blister atop the third toe of his right foot. Before long, the boy began to feel ill and ran a fever. Signs of a blood infection appeared, but despite doctors' best efforts, young Calvin, Jr., was dead within a week.

Sixteen-year-old Calvin, Jr., died of sepsis, even though his father was one of the most powerful people on earth, because he did not have access to today's common antibiotics such as penicillin.

Regarding healthcare costs, we can isolate one sector of the industry which is not covered by insurance policies, and far less regulated by the state, as in the case with elective LASIK eye surgery. According to the Foundation for Economic Education:

> Between the late 1990s and 2016, the cost of hospital and related services in the US rose by more than 177 percent. This has sparked concern, and rightfully so, that too many Americans are going without care due to skyrocketing costs.
>
> The cost of LASIK surgery, on the other hand, has dropped by 44 percent over the years. In 1998, when LASIK was becoming more common in the US, it cost a patient about $2,500 per eye. Adjusted for inflation, that would be about $4,000 per eye in today's economy.
>
> In 2019, the cost of LASIK surgery performed in the US is about $2,246 per eye. In 2018, that cost was lower, at around $2,199 per eye, but when we compare this slight increase to the 177 percent increase across the board on healthcare costs, it's clear to see that whatever model LASIK has adopted is working.[52]

The Imperialism Myth and the Slavery Myth

Two historically fallacious ideas pose stumbling blocks to appreciating how the freedom to trade voluntarily and contract create wealth in society: the Imperialism Myth and the Slavery Myth.

Claim: Wealthy countries are wealthy because they have stolen resources through conquest against other exploited countries.

Reality: Empires benefit special interests within a country, not the country as a whole. Tell a Progressive that all Americans have benefited from the invasion of Afghanistan, Iraq, Syria, Libya, Pakistan, and Yemen — you'll be met with laughter. One can clearly see that politicians and defense contractors have benefited greatly, but only at the expense of the population at large. The same concept holds true for imperialism in the past.

Claim: Wealthy countries are wealthy because they were built on the backs of slave (or free) labor.

Reality: One of the oldest legal texts known to the human race is *The Code of Ur-Nammu* (c. 2100–2050 BCE) from Mesopotamia. The text mentions "slave" nine times. It turns out that slavery was around long before any significant increases in wealth, and it is the least unique thing about Western Civilization. How can an institution which has existed on every continent except Antarctica since the beginning of time be the cause of wealth in some areas only recently?

We can falsify this position by looking at economic wealth that existed before and after the abolition of slavery in certain geographical areas, and determining whether a correlation exists between concentrations of slavery and wealth. It turns out that countries like England and America became wealthier after abolishing slavery. If the thesis were correct, we would have seen their wealth drastically increasing under slavery and then plummeting after abolition.

Second, we can compare the wealth of the American South (where slavery was much more prevalent) to the American North. Both in the past and today the average Northern American had higher incomes than the average Southern American.[53]

As Thomas Sowell explains in *Black Rednecks and White Liberals*:

> In many parts of the non-Western world, slaves were sources of domestic amenities and means of displaying wealth with an impressive retinue, rather than sources of wealth. Often they were a drain on the wealth already possessed. According to a scholarly study of slavery in China, the slaves there "did not generate any surplus; they consumed it." Another study concluded: "The Middle East and the Arab world rarely used slaves for productive activities." Even though some slaveowners — those whose slaves produced commercial crops or other saleable products — received wealth from the fruits of the unpaid labor of these slaves, that is very different

from saying that the society as a whole, or even its non-slave population as a whole, ended up wealthier than it would have been in the absence of slavery.[54]

Slave labor is sometimes referred to as "free" labor.

The lack of monetary compensation of work distracts from the fact that what made slavery immoral was that the labor being performed was involuntary.

Either way, owning slaves was by no means "free." Slave owners bought slaves at auction and then paid for their housing, food, shelter, and clothing. According to Frederick Douglass, a former slave:

> Here, too, the slaves of all the other farms received their monthly *allowance* of food, and their yearly clothing. The men and women slaves received, as their monthly *allowance* of food, eight pounds of pork, or its equivalent in fish, and one bushel of corn meal. Their yearly clothing consisted of two coarse linen shirts, one pair of linen trousers, like the shirts, one jacket, one pair of trousers for winter, made of coarse negro cloth, one pair of stockings, and one pair of shoes; the whole of which could not have cost more than seven dollars. The *allowance* of the slave children was given to their mothers, or the old women having the care of them. The children unable to work in the field had neither shoes, stockings, jackets, nor trousers, given to them; their clothing consisted of two coarse linen shirts per year. When these failed them, they went naked until the next *allowance*-day. Children from seven to ten years old, of both sexes, almost naked, might be seen at all seasons of the year.[55] (emphasis mine)

To be clear, slavery (forced labor of innocent people) is immoral, regardless of the monetary cost. The point here is to refute the mindset that slave labor was "free" and thus the engine of American economic growth.

Again, focusing on the lack of monetary compensation distracts from the lack of consent, which is at the root of why slavery is immoral. Ignoring this distinction allows Progressives to be unbothered by the forced labor of military conscription, a far more dangerous and deadly job than forced cotton-picking.

These (ahistorical) narratives — or prevailing interpretations of past events — shape how people in the present think issues should be addressed.

Poverty is mankind's natural state. What needs to be explained is why some nations are wealthy.

The one thing that differentiates wealthy nations from impoverished nations is the widespread recognition of the private property ethic. This includes private property to encourage investment, freedom of trade/exchange/contract, and stable governance.

This explains why West Germany was wealthier than East Germany, why South Korea is wealthier than North Korea, and why Botswana is wealthier than Zimbabwe; why China's economy grew after liberalization in the late 1970s after the death of Mao; and why India experienced significant growth after liberalization in 1991. The wealthiest countries clearly correlate with high degrees of economic freedom. Hong Kong and Singapore were rated first and second in the 2020 Index of Economic Freedom published by the Heritage Foundation and *Wall Street Journal*. The citizens of both countries have higher standards of living as compared to citizens of neighboring countries which have implemented less-free economic models.

Side note: The Nordic Countries, which Bernie Sanders often says are examples of socialism, rank higher than the United States on the same Index of Economic Freedom.

In short, wealthy countries are wealthy because they allow significantly more freedom to contract voluntarily between consenting adults.

As summarized by historian Niall Ferguson in his book *Civilization: The West and the Rest*:

> Institutions are, of course, in some sense the products of culture. But, because they formalize a set of norms, institutions are often the things that keep a culture honest, determining how far it is conducive to good behavior rather than bad. To illustrate the point, the twentieth century ran a series of experiments, imposing quite different institutions on two sets of *Germans (in West and East)*, two sets of *Koreans (in North and South)* and two sets of *Chinese (inside and outside the People's Republic)*. The results were very striking and the lesson crystal clear. *If you take the same people, with more or less the same culture, and impose communist institutions on one group and capitalist institutions on another, almost immediately there will be a divergence in the way they behave.*
>
> Many historians today would agree that there were few really profound differences between the eastern and western ends of Eurasia in the 1500s. Both regions were early adopters of agriculture, market-based exchange and urban-centred state structures. But there was one crucial institutional difference. In China a monolithic empire had been consolidated, while Europe remained politically fragmented. In *Guns, Germs and Steel*, Jared Diamond explained why Eurasia had advanced ahead of the rest of the world. But not until his essay "How to Get Rich" (1999) did he offer an answer to the question of why one end of Eurasia forged so far ahead of the other. The answer was that, in the plains of Eastern Eurasia, monolithic

> Oriental empires stifled innovation, while in mountainous, river-divided Western Eurasia, multiple monarchies and city-states engaged in creative competition and communication.[56] (emphasis mine)

When it comes to measuring wealth within a society, the best place to look is not at the wealthiest people, but to gauge the opportunities available to those with the lowest incomes.

Taking the example of America, we can test the hypothesis of the Progressive claim that "the rich get richer and the poor get poorer." By comparing the income of the average 16-year-old first-time jobholder with the average income of the same person at age 46 (after years of experience and an increase in skills), we can judge whether the poor are getting wealthier over time. If Progressive orthodoxy is correct, the average 46-year-old will have a lower income because "the poor get poorer."

Of course, we see the opposite. The average annual income of a 16-year-old in America is $31,668, while the average 46-year-old earns $63,648 per year.[57] As people gain more on-the-job skills, they can demand higher wages as businesses compete for their talent stack. Free market economists have explained this for decades, while Progressives continue to reject the science.

The statistical trickery comes into play when Progressives judge groups of people, in place of measuring the wealth of human beings. You might hear: "The bottom 20 percent of earners have seen no wage growth in the last 30 years when adjusted for inflation."

This is akin to the following fallacy:

> Bob is doing research on university admissions in the year 2010. In 2010, he noticed the average age of freshmen at this university was 18. Ten years later, in 2020, Bob returned to the university, and found that the average freshman age was still 18 years old. Therefore, Bob concludes that students at this university do not age.

Notice the fallacious thinking. "Freshmen" is a group of humans, a group which people enter and exit after a short while, just as "bottom 20 percent of income earners" is a group people are only temporarily in, and then will most likely move out of.

According to Thomas Sowell:

> [A] University of Michigan study found that, among working Americans who were in the bottom 20 percent in income in 1975, approximately 95 percent had risen out of that bracket by 1991 — including 29 percent who had reached the top quintile by 1991,

compared to only 5 percent who still remained in the bottom quintile...

The IRS found that between 1996 and 2005 the income of individuals who had been in the bottom 20 percent of income tax filers in 1996 had increased by 91 percent by 2005, and the income of those individuals who were in the top one percent in 1996 had fallen by 26 percent...

Even among the truly rich, there is turnover. When *Forbes* magazine ran its first list of the 400 richest Americans in 1982, that list included 14 Rockefellers, 28 du Ponts and 11 Hunts. Twenty years later, the list included 3 Rockefellers, one Hunt and no du Ponts. Just over one fifth of the people on the 1982 *Forbes* list of the wealthiest Americans inherited their wealth. By 2006, however, only two percent of the people on the list had inherited their wealth...

When the incomes of people making $50,000 or less fell by 2 percent between 2007 and 2009, the incomes of people making a million dollars or more fell by nearly 50 percent.[58]

Another method of measuring income mobility is to ignore monetary measures frequently clouded by inflation, and to look instead at the time-price. This is *the amount of time an average worker has to perform labor in order to obtain a product or service. Superabundance: The Story of Population Growth, Innovation, and Human Flourishing on an Infinitely Bountiful Planet* (2022) by Marian Tupy and Gale Pooley reveals that the average worker today spends significantly less time than previous generations in order to access such items as pork, rice, coffee, computers, phones, televisions, clothes, and lighting. Even resources like rubber, cotton, steel, oil, and aluminum have fallen in terms of time-price by more than 90 percent. While people seldom purchase these products directly, the lower prices of these goods lower the costs of production, making resulting products more affordable for the masses.

We can therefore look at goods and services which were previously out of reach for the layman, and see whether he has more or less access to those products in more recent times.

The following chart (which I discovered in Stephen Moore's *Who's the Fairest of Them All? The Truth About Opportunity, Taxes, and Wealth in America*[59]) indicates that the average poor person in 2005 had more access to basic goods and services than did the average person in 1970:

Percent of Households that own:	All Households, 1970	Poor, 2005
Washing machine	71	72
Clothes Dryer	44	57
Dishwasher	19	37
Refrigerator	83	99
Stove	87	99
Microwave	1	73
Color TV	40	97
Videocassette/DVD	1	78
Personal Computer	1	78
Telephone	93	96
Cell Phone	1	60
Air Conditioner	34	82

Dallas Federal Reserve, based on Census Bureau data

Similar findings come from Ronald Bailey and Marian L. Tupy's *Ten Global Trends Every Smart Person Should Know*[60]:

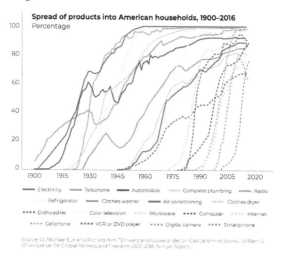

If the Progressive theory of "the poor get poorer" were true, we would see the opposite outcome.

For example, even air travel has become more accessible to the average person over time. According to Airlines for America, in 1971, only 49 percent of Americans had flown commercially. By 2022, that number was 87 percent. Few, if any, Progressives would have predicted this after the Airline Deregulation Act of 1978.

Having a third party involve itself coercively in areas of the economy puts more costly barriers between producers and consumers, making the poorest among us worse off in the end.

Coercive economic regulation, whether foreign (i.e., sanctions, tariffs, or embargoes) or domestic, harms the most vulnerable people in society.

9. How Could Anyone Be an Anarchist?

After abandoning Progressivism, I realized that I was against the existence of a state because it necessarily violates the principles of self-ownership and social cooperation. But how could anyone support the libertarian anarchist alternative? The following are transcript excerpts from the *Don't Tread on Anyone* podcast:

Keith Knight: A lot of criticism of the free market is not unique to the free market. For example, there is greed, there is dog-eat-dog competition, it can disrupt and disorder, and there's no guarantee of my safety.

Well, that all applies tenfold to the state because you can't opt out of funding them and they have no competition. Do you think there's anything that uniquely applies negatively to the free market that justifies the existence of the state?

Art Carden: I really don't think there is. I tend to believe that states are kind of inevitable and there's always going to be an organization with a comparative advantage in violence — that's the way that my advisor defined a state when I was in graduate school — but I don't think it's necessary.

Sort of like the song… where the girl's singing, "Anything you can do, I can do better," I would say that anything states can do, markets do better. I don't think the state is necessary for any of the problems that we want to fix or any of the problems that we want to solve. I think the last four years have been a really nice illustration of the difference between the market and the state when you consider the administration of Donald Trump.

A lot of people are horrified at Donald Trump as just a crass human being who is just an opportunist. Assume for the sake of argument that everything everybody says about Trump is right, that he's the worst of the worst. Okay, well, would you prefer a world in which he's doing suspect real estate deals in New Jersey and New York to a world in which he has his finger on the nuclear button? I think the answer is yes. I would much rather Donald Trump confine his efforts to trying to make money in the real estate market than try to make America great again by pursuing all sorts of boneheaded policies like immigration restrictions and tariffs.

* * * *

Keith Knight: In your books *Political Philosophy: An Introduction* and *Why Not Capitalism?*, you mention this excellent book, *The Problem of Political Authority: An Examination of the Right to Coerce and the Duty to Obey* by Michael Huemer. What is so important about this book?

Jason Brennan: Yeah, that is one of my favorite books. One of the main questions in political philosophy is: What, if anything, justifies government? In particular, governments claim to have two special moral powers — I'm going to use different words than the ones he uses — I call them legitimacy and authority.

"Legitimacy" refers to a supposed governmental power to create and enforce rules over a certain geographic area against certain people. So, governments are a proper subset of a society which claim the right to have monopoly power in coercively enforcing rules. That's what they are.

So, what makes government legitimate? If anything, why would it have the right to create these rules? Why would it be allowed to enforce rules that others cannot?

"Authority" is another purported power of government. To have authority is to have a power to impose on another an obligation to obey. If I say to you right now, "You may not smoke marijuana," you don't think you have any obligation to follow my orders, right? If I say, "I order you not to smoke pot," you're like, "Who are you? I don't have to listen to you." But when governments order us not to smoke pot, most people believe that we acquire an obligation not to do it in virtue of government issuing that order.

It's really perplexing. Why would government have legitimacy? Why would it have authority? What Mike does in that book is he very carefully goes through a couple thousand years of arguments trying to show that governments have authority and legitimacy, and it's amazing how bad these arguments are. Basically, they all fail.

The argument that you get in middle school that your teachers tell you is: "Well, government has authority because you consent to government." No, you don't. There's no plausible interpretation of the relationship between you and your government under which there's consent. They'll make other kinds of arguments as well, so Mike very carefully goes through and shows that none of these arguments work. He then gives us a psychological diagnosis about why we might believe in government authority, even though we don't have any good arguments on its behalf. That's the first half. The first half just basically shows we don't have any reason to believe in authority or legitimacy.

The second half then asks: Is anarchism feasible? If we don't have reason to believe in authority or legitimacy, what about the alternative — anarchism? And Mike says, we don't know if it would work, maybe it would be a disaster, but he gives us some grounds for thinking empirically that it would work better than people think. A lot of the things they think would happen under anarchy, it's not as bad as they think.

Some other books you might read on that — if you're interested in anarchism — there's a book called *Anarchy Unbound* which is a nice case study in how anarchism [might work]. Actually, the subtitle is "Why Self-Governance Works Better Than You Think." There's another book by Edward Stringham called *Private Governance*, where he points out that, as a matter of fact, this is an empirical claim that... the rule-enforcing that protects your rights in your own life is not done by government; it's done through extralegal channels.

* * * *

Keith Knight: It's incredible that he can be so skeptical about market failure but doesn't hold those same principles to the state. The argument is that people don't have tons of information in the market, so they make bad decisions. What, are people omniscient about politics and politicians? "Well," they'll say, "There's greed in the marketplace." But there's greed in politics!

Do you see anything that applies to the free market in a unique way that is negative and unique to the market, that doesn't apply to the state tenfold? Considering you can't opt out of funding them and they don't have competitors?

Bryan Caplan: That's a tough question. It's a good one. Let me come back to that in just a minute.

Here's what was very revealing to me about Paul Krugman. Tyler Cowen did an interview with him, and Tyler was able to ask him some really hard questions about why exactly he would think the government would do well. Here's the thing: Paul Krugman doesn't think the governments do well. When you actually get him on that topic, he says, "Yeah, this government really screwed up."

Tyler actually had what to me is the million-dollar question. He said, "You're very partisan, Paul. You really hate the Republicans. You really like the Democrats. Yet if we look at a bunch of states where they have one-party Democratic rule, you're not happy with what they've done. So, dude, what gives?" And Paul did not dodge the question. He did have some thoughts (that weren't satisfactory), but he did acknowledge the issue. He even said, "Yeah, well, you know, in your one-party Democratic states you wind up getting a lot of good old boys' clubs. They're kind of corrupt, and they don't really worry about pleasing voters anymore. Sometimes you get a pragmatic Republican governor in the Northeast and that works out maybe better, but let's not quite say that." That was the gist of it.

To me it really comes down to, at a core level: Can you just say, "I just think the government is going to mess it up," or is it just a matter of "It has messed up a bunch of times, but there's no general lesson"? In other words, someone like Paul Krugman is happy to admit the government has screwed up a bunch of times, but he doesn't want to draw as a lesson that we should expect government to keep screwing up in similar ways in the future. He wants to think of that as accidental. For him, government failure is more accidental — it just happened — whereas market failure is systematic; it's the way the system works. If you were to say, "Well, that's the way the government works, too," it would be very hard for him to deal with that. He does dodge that, but he's not blind. He's a super smart guy, and when you frame it in the right way, he does acknowledge things you might be surprised he acknowledges. That was one of my favorite encounters — I wasn't there — but it was one of my favorite expressions of the way that he thinks.

In terms of problems that markets have that governments don't have ten times over, probably the best answer is the problem of transaction costs. The key thing about markets is: to make things happen, you've got to get people to agree. Sometimes that is so expensive that there's just no way to accomplish it. Government basically has the ability to pull out a gun and say, "We're going to save a lot of money on the negotiation now because we're just going to do it my way. Shut up." That causes a bunch of other problems, but it does save on negotiation costs.

Knight: All right. I'll give that one to you. But for the same reason, we wouldn't say, "Negotiation costs are high; therefore, the Koch brothers have the right to initiate aggression against peaceful people." Well, we shouldn't give it to Doug Ducey or Donald Trump either.

Caplan: Yeah, I agree, but that's still the kind of thing I would point to.

Knight: Excellent, thank you.

$* * * *$

Keith Knight: I'll often ask people: "If I don't like what Olive Garden is doing, can I stop working there or going there?" Or, what if I said the same about Walmart? People look at me and say, "Obviously. Of course you have the right to stop funding them." However, when it comes to government services, people don't extend that same courtesy. How is it that people understand government to be held to a totally different moral standard from all other organizations?

Jason Brennan: I work a great length on political psychology, and a lot of my work is on thinking about what political psychology tells us about the justification of democracy and voting behavior. In general, what political psychologists find is that most people don't really have an ideology, and they don't really have strong political beliefs.

The people who do, for most of them, it's kind of a post hoc rationalization. Where the model is almost — this would be sort of personal to me — it's like you're an Irish guy from Northern Massachusetts. Irish guys from Northern Massachusetts tend to vote Democrat, not because there's anything special about the Democrats helping them, but just because that's what people like us do in the same way that you root for the Patriots, right? Then a small percentage of those people will then post hoc rationalize that they agree with the beliefs of their party.

So, when you look at what people believe about politics, you can't really get too excited by that. As Robin Hanson would say, the purpose of politics is not policy. Politics is not about policy. People's political beliefs are not about describing how they think the world really works or should work. Rather, we use our political beliefs in the same way that we use t-shirts. It's a way of showing certain people that I'm on their side and part of their coalition. The fact that there's an inconsistency in most people's beliefs is not surprising because they're not using those beliefs to form a rational theory about the world. They're using them for another social purpose.

But you're right, there is a huge tension there. The reasons that people give against socially mandatory monopoly... Why would it be bad if Walmart were the only retailer, and you were forced to shop at Walmart? If there were no permission to have competition, they're going to give you some account for that. If you ask them the same question, "Why doesn't your antimonopoly argument apply to government?" It's not clear how they overcome that.

The main thing they're going to say is: "We have to have a monopoly on violence. Violence is different. Governments enforce the rules with violence, and if we had competition, what that would mean is that we'd have warring factions on the street constantly fighting. Police Force A and Police Force B would be shooting each other to try to maintain dominance."

Is that true? Well, again, if you would look at *Anarchy Unbound* by Peter Leeson and Mike Huemer's book *The Problem of Political Authority* to give you an account of why this view of anarchy is probably not right; anarchism would not mean just constant violence on the streets between warring factions and gangs.

* * * *

Keith Knight: A lot of criticism of the free market, you'll hear things like, "Well, there's corruption, there's greed, and people don't have a lot of information, so they often get manipulated."

The problem with virtually all of these criticisms is they apply tenfold to government intervention because you can't opt out of it, and they don't face competitors to which you can go to if you're not satisfied with their product or service. Do you see that there's any unique criticism of the free market that doesn't also apply to socialism or the state?

Johan Norberg: Now, what would that be? I mean, the corruption thing, definitely. If you have to go to eleven bureaucrats to start a business or get your permit or your license requirement, that's eleven bureaucrats who can force you to pay bribes to do it. That's one of the biggest problems in many poor countries. When I've been to Kenya, people tell me in the slums that they have a saying that it's not safe to carry cash around here because there are too many policemen. The policemen, they say, "Oh, you got a store here. It would be sad if something happened to that. You don't have a permit, right? Pay up." So, the fewer restrictions and regulations, the fewer opportunities for corruption.

Is there anything unique you can say about the problems of free markets that doesn't apply to [the state]? They would have to be more, I think, psychological. It would have to be something about: Are we overwhelmed with choice? Perhaps we don't want as much freedom as we have in a more open economy. Perhaps it's better if someone tells us what to do. I think there are some intellectuals who are trying to make that argument.

Knight: Well, we have Cass Sunstein who wrote the book *Nudge* where he says that, yeah, unfortunately, people have too much choice, and it's the role of the state to coerce them into doing otherwise.

But for the same reason I oppose the state forcibly stopping me, I also oppose Walmart from stopping me, and Amazon. I hold them to the same standard I'd hold anyone else. Maybe choice is bad, but that doesn't give me the right to go around violently dominating Johan Norberg. Like, I'm going to need to see a copy of the book before I allow it to be published because you have too many choices with what you want to write about.

Norberg: Yeah, it's always the other guy's choices that's a problem, right? It's never your own that have to be restricted.

Quotes

The following is a collection of miscellaneous quotes which I have come across in researching which led me to believe that Progressivism was an immoral, ahistorical, economically illiterate worldview.

If the government didn't have a monopoly on security, only rich people would be able to have security just like when the government got out of other businesses, the only cars produced were limousines, the only clothes produced were tuxedos and the only food produced was foie gras.

– Michael Malice

I plead for greater liberty and a more open world, not because I believe one system happens to be more efficient than another, but because those things provide a setting that unleashes individual creativity as no other system can. They spur dynamism that has led to human, economic, scientific, and technological advances... At its core, belief in capitalism is belief in mankind... My aim is freedom and voluntary relations in all fields.

– Johan Norberg, *In Defense of Global Capitalism*

To kill one man is to be guilty of a capital crime, to kill ten men is to increase the guilt tenfold, to kill a hundred men is to increase it a hundredfold. This the rulers of the earth all recognize, and yet when it comes to the greatest crime — waging war on another state — they praise it!... If a man on seeing a little black were to say it is black, but on seeing a lot of black were to say it is white, it would be clear that such a man could not distinguish black and white... So those who recognize a small crime as such, but do not recognize the wickedness of the greatest crime of all... cannot distinguish right and wrong.

– Mozi (470–391 B.C.), *Condemnation of Offensive War I*, Book V

The progress of civilization has meant the reduction of employment, not its increase. It is because we have become increasingly wealthy as a nation that we have been able to virtually eliminate child labor.

– Henry Hazlitt, *Economics in One Lesson*

[I]f this were truly a "white supremacist" society, being called a white supremacist would be a badge of honor, not a professional death sentence.

– Thomas E. Woods, Jr.

Private property isn't about selfishness so much as it's about creative control. Someone might want to have their own business, not because they're greedy, but because they have a vision of how they want things to go that won't be realized if everyone else gets a say in it.

– Chris Freiman, Professor, John Chambers College of Business and Economics at WVU

Quick objection to socialism. Just as some students thrive in group projects and others don't, some workers thrive in cooperatives and others don't. So we shouldn't insist that *every* workplace be collectivized in some way; let workers choose whatever arrangement suits them best.

– Chris Freiman

Some people might say, "Well, the problem is, if we can sell kidneys, then really desperately poor people would sell their kidneys — and richer people wouldn't — and you'd exploit them." Part of my response is to say, "If you have a person who's in such dire straits that their best option is to sell a kidney, and you take that away from them, you're a horrible human being who doesn't care about social justice. Your moral sense is completely warped, I hope you're not voting." It's a forceful thing to say, but it's true… this is a horrible thing for that human being to have to do, but also it's their best option, which means if you take that away, they're gonna do something even worse than that.

– Jason Brennan, Professor and author of *Markets Without Limits*, from an episode of Keith Knight's *Don't Tread on Anyone* podcast.

Against the broader background of world history, however, a very different lesson might be that no people of any color can be trusted with unbridled power over any other people, for such power has been grossly abused by whatever race, class, or political authority has held that power, whether under ancient despotism or modern totalitarianism, as well as under serfdom, slavery, or other forms of oppression.

It was not because people thought slavery was right that it persisted for thousands of years. It persisted largely because people did not think about the rightness or wrongness of it at all.

– Thomas Sowell, Black Rednecks and White Liberals

The state represents violence in a concentrated and organized form. The Individual has a soul, but as the state is a soulless machine, it can never be weaned from violence to which it owes its very existence.

– Mahatma Gandhi, "Interview with Nirmal Kumar Bose,"
November 9–10, 1934, Modern Review (October 1935 Edition).

… Sam **Walton**, the founder of Walmart, became one of the wealthiest men in the world by figuring out how to cut the price of just about everything to the benefit of everyone, but especially of lower-income consumers. That's one of the other virtues of the free market: it rewards people who can figure out how to supply products and services that might have originally only been affordable to the wealthy so cheaply that just about anyone can afford and enjoy them. Henry **Ford** became wealthy by producing cheaper and cheaper (and better and better quality) automobiles; John D. **Rockefeller** became wealthy by selling refined kerosene and other oil industry products cheaper and cheaper for decades; Cornelius **Vanderbilt** got his start in business by managing a steamship business on the Hudson River in which the ride was free (!), making money by selling food and drinks on board; and on and on.

For their efforts such men have been denigrated by the enemies of economic freedom (including various politicians, government bureaucrats, socialist ideologues in academe, journalism, and elsewhere) as "robber barons." Of course, they did not "rob" anyone.

Unlike government, **they could not force anyone to buy their products; they had to persuade people to buy them by making them cheaper and better.** Only government can rob you of your hard-earned money by threatening imprisonment for refusal to pay what it demands of you for services or products that you may have no need for whatsoever, and whose existence you may even deeply resent. It's called tax evasion, a crime that is punished under federal and state law by fines, imprisonment, or both…

That is why the most menial local government tax-collecting bureaucrat can have more power over your life than the wealthiest businessperson in the world. Businesspeople must persuade people to purchase more of their products or services; unelected government bureaucrats can order you to shut down your business, take your kids out of school, or quit your job, and get the police to enforce the orders (as all Americans learned during the pandemic of 2020–2022).

– Thomas J. DiLorenzo,
The Politically Incorrect Guide to Economics

The standard theory of monopoly within the mainstream of the economics profession is that monopolies increase prices and reduce production levels compared to competitive industries. So I gathered historical economic data on prices and production for seventeen of the industries accused of monopolization during the congressional debates over the Sherman Act. Surprisingly, no other economist had apparently ever done this! What I found was that while real (inflation-adjusted) gross domestic product (GDP) increased by about 24 percent from 1880 to 1890, the industries accused of "restricting output" increased their production by 175 percent on average, seven times more than the economy in general. For example, steel production rose by 258 percent, zinc 156 percent, coal 153 percent, steel rails 142 percent, petroleum 79 percent, and sugar 75 percent. And during that same time period, as the consumer price index (CPI) fell by 7 percent, the "trusts" that were accused of monopolization dropped their prices by far more. The price of steel rail fell by 53 percent, refined sugar became 22 percent cheaper, lead declined in price by 12 percent, and zinc by 20 percent, for example. This trend of production in these industries dominated by "trusts" — the supposed "natural monopolies" — outstripping GDP as a whole and prices declining faster in these industries than the CPI continued on for the next decade as well.

– Thomas J. DiLorenzo,
The Politically Incorrect Guide to Economics

My case for pacifism, to recap, comes down to three simple premises. The first two are empirical:

Premise #1: The short-run costs of war are clearly awful. [Empirical claim about immediate effects of war].

Premise #2: The long-run benefits of war are highly uncertain. [Empirical claim about people's ability to accurately forecast the long-run effects of war].

These empirical claims imply pacifism when combined with a bland moral premise:

Premise #3: For a war to be morally justified, the expected long-run benefits have to substantially exceed its short-run costs. [Moral claim, inspired by Judith Jarvis Thomson's forced organ donation hypothetical].

– Bryan Caplan, *How Evil Are Politicians?: Essays on Demagoguery*

There is also a prima facie similarity between the democratic idea of citizens controlling the government through their votes, and the capitalist idea of customers controlling companies through their purchasing decisions. Both politicians and businesspeople have to cater to the masses.

The difference, again, is that the capitalist idea is the version that actually makes sense. You actually have an incentive to pay attention and figure out which company is best, because then you can actually get that company's product. By contrast, as discussed previously, voters have no such incentive. However diligent and rational you are in your voting decisions, you still get whatever the majority of other people vote for, so there's no point wasting time trying to figure out who the best candidate is.

This explains why markets tend to be much more responsive to consumers than governments are. (If you haven't noticed that, try calling up a government agency some time, tell them you're very unhappy with their services and you want a refund. See how far you get.)

– Michael Huemer, *Privatize Law and Order*

Here's the one sentence argument for utilitarian libertarianism: compared with other institutions, markets do the best job of promoting social happiness without depending on people trying to promote social happiness. Markets solve two major problems for utilitarianism. First, most people don't desire to maximize social happiness as opposed to their own happiness and the happiness of a relatively small circle of family and friends. Second, even if people desire to maximize social happiness, they generally don't know how. As individuals, we know very little about the distribution of the world's resources and particular people's desires for those resources. Consequently, we lack the information we need to produce an optimal match between resources and people. But markets provide both the incentives and the information that people need to advance the happiness of strangers. Markets generally make our moral and cognitive limitations work for us rather than against us. They channel self-interest toward the public interest.

– Chris Freiman, *Arguments for Liberty*

Listing the main ways that society appears to treat men less fairly than women requires only a little more reflection to complete. Topping the list:

a. Men are overrepresented at the bottom levels of society. They do most of the nasty, dangerous work, are much more likely to be homeless or imprisoned, and much more likely to **kill themselves**.

b. Men spend much more **time on the job** than women.

c. The law heavily favors women in child **custody** and child support disputes.

d. Men are more likely to be **victims** of violent crime.

e. Men are much more likely to die in combat; in fact, during serious military conflicts, they face **military slavery** ("the draft").

f. Women view men as "**success objects**."

– Bryan Caplan, "Don't Be a Feminist: Essays on Genuine Justice"

Free markets are awesome because they give business incentives to do good stuff that sounds bad. Governments are awful because they give politicians incentives to do bad stuff that sounds good. Since the correlation between what IS good and what SOUNDS good is quite low, this is a huge deal.

– Bryan Caplan

The rapid economic advance that we have come to expect seems in a large measure to be the result of this inequality and to be impossible without it. Progress at such a fast rate cannot proceed on a uniform front but must take place in echelon fashion...

At any stage of this process there will always be many things we already know how to produce but which are still too expensive to provide for more than a few...

All the conveniences of a comfortable home, of our means of transportation and communication, of entertainment and enjoyment, we could produce at first only in limited quantities; but it was in doing this that we gradually learned to make them or similar things at a much smaller outlay of resources and thus became able to supply them to the great majority. A large part of the expenditure of the rich, though not intended for that end, thus serves to defray the cost of the experimentation with the new things that, as a result, can later be made available to the poor.

– F.A. Hayek, *The Constitution of Liberty*

Mutual aid was particularly popular among the poor and the working class. For instance, in New York City in 1909, 40 percent of families earning less than $1,000 a year, little more than the "living wage," had members who were in mutual-aid societies. Ethnicity, however, was an even greater predictor of mutual-aid membership than income. The "new immigrants," such as the Germans, Bohemians, and Russians, many of whom were Jews, participated in mutual-aid societies at approximately twice the rate of native whites and six times the rate of the Irish… By the 1920s, at least one out of every three males was a member of a mutual-aid society. Members of societies carried over $9 billion worth of life insurance by 1920. During the same period, "lodges dominated the field of health insurance." Numerous lodges offered unemployment benefits. Some black fraternal lodges, taking note of the sporadic nature of African American employment at the time, allowed members to receive unemployment benefits even if they were up to six months behind in dues…Under lodge medicine, the price for healthcare was low. Members typically paid $2, about a day's wage, to have yearly access to a doctor's care (minor surgery was frequently included in this fee). Non-lodge members typically paid about $2 every doctor's visit during this time period.

— Joshua Fulton, *Welfare Before the Welfare State*

The real bosses, in the capitalist system of market economy, are the consumers: They, by their buying and by their abstention from buying, decide who should own the capital and run the plants. They determine what should be produced and in what quantity and quality. Their attitudes result either in profit or in loss for the enterpriser. They make poor men rich and rich men poor. They are no easy bosses.

— Ludwig von Mises, *Bureaucracy*

The bourgeoisie, during its rule of scarce one hundred years, has created more massive and more colossal productive forces than have all preceding generations together. Subjection of Nature's forces to man, machinery, application of chemistry to industry and agriculture, steam-navigation, railways, electric telegraphs, clearing of whole continents for cultivation, canalisation of rivers, whole populations conjured out of the ground — what earlier century had even a presentiment that such productive forces slumbered in the lap of social labour?

— Karl Marx & Frederick Engels, *The Communist Manifesto*

What makes wages rise and renders the material conditions of the wage earners more satisfactory is improvement in the technological equipment. American wages are higher than wages in other countries because the capital invested per head of the worker is greater and the plants are thereby in the position to use the most efficient tools and machines.

What is called the American way of life is the result of the fact that the United States has put fewer obstacles in the way of saving and capital accumulation than other nations...

There is only one way that leads to an improvement of the standard of living for the wage-earning masses, viz., the increase in the amount of capital invested.

– Ludwig von Mises, *Planning for Freedom and*
Sixteen Other Essays and Addresses

[T]he number of blacks in professional, technical, and other high-level occupations more than doubled in the decade preceding the Civil Rights Act of 1964. In other occupations, gains by blacks were greater during the 1940s — when there was practically no civil rights legislation — than during the 1950s. In various skilled trades, the income of blacks relative to whites more than doubled between 1936 and 1959...

Affirmative action hiring pressures make it costly to have no minority employees, but continuing affirmative action pressures at the promotion and discharge phases also make it costly to have minority employees who do not work out well. The net effect is to increase the demand for highly qualified minority employees while decreasing the demand for less qualified minority employees or for those without a sufficient track record to reassure employers."

– Thomas Sowell, *Civil Rights: Rhetoric or Reality?*

"Won't the Mafia take over?"

It is paradoxical that the fear of rule by organized crime families causes people to support the State, which is the most "organized" and criminal association in human history. Even if it were true that under market anarchy, people had to pay protection money and occasionally get whacked, this would be a drop in the bucket compared to the taxation and wartime deaths caused by governments. But even this concedes too much. For the mob derives its strength from government, not the free market. All of the businesses traditionally associated with organized crime — gambling, prostitution, loan sharking, drug dealing — are prohibited or heavily regulated by the State. In market anarchy, true professionals would drive out such unscrupulous competitors.

– Robert P. Murphy, *Chaos Theory*

Capitalism is essentially a system of mass production for the satisfaction of the needs of the masses. It pours a horn of plenty upon the common man. It has raised the average standard of living to a height never dreamed of in earlier ages. It has made accessible to millions of people enjoyments which a few generations ago were only within the reach of a small elite.

– Ludwig von Mises, *The Anti-Capitalist Mentality*

The socialist society would have to **forbid** capitalist acts between **consenting adults**.

– Robert Nozick, *Anarchy, State, and Utopia*

We do not usually make people better off by reducing their alternatives.

– David D. Friedman, *Hidden Order:*
The Economics of Everyday Life

Knowledge of the strengths of blacks has been ignored or repressed in a different way as well. Few people today are aware that the ghettos in many cities were far safer places two generations ago than they are today, both for blacks and for whites. Incredulity often greets stories by older blacks as to their habit of sleeping out on fire escapes or on rooftops or in public parks on hot summer nights. Many of those same people would not dare to walk through those same parks today in broad daylight. In the 1930s whites went regularly to Harlem at night, stayed until the wee hours of the morning, and then stood on the streets to hail cabs to take them home. Today, not only would very few whites dare to do this, very few cabs would dare to be cruising ghetto streets in the wee hours of the morning.

Why should discussion of positive achievements by blacks ever be a source of embarrassment, much less resentment, on the part of black leaders? Because many of these positive achievements occurred in ways that completely undermine the civil rights vision. If crime is a product of poverty and discrimination as they say endlessly, why was there so much less of it when poverty and discrimination were much worse than today?

If massive programs are the only hope to reduce violence in the ghetto, why was there so much less violence long before anyone ever thought of these programs?

– Thomas Sowell, *Civil Rights: Rhetoric or Reality?*

… [T]he reason we're richer now than we were in the past is of course not because we have more resources — if anything, we have fewer. Instead, it's because we are more knowledgeable about how best to employ existing resources. But, typically, when we learn how to make something new, such as a cellular phone, it is very expensive to produce it on a per-unit basis. The rich buy the first units, get all of the benefits at first, but then also pay all of the up-front costs. They thereby pay for the basic infrastructure that makes it available for all. The rich pay for experimentation and innovation and fund entrepreneurs in finding ways to market to the poor, though this is not the intention of the rich. The reason wealthy countries today can provide what used to be luxuries (TVs, electricity, flush toilets) for all is because in the past those countries allowed such goods to be provided for just a few, rather than prohibited because not all can have them.

– Jason Brennan, *Why It's OK to Want to Be Rich*

If human beings are so careless, stupid and malicious that they cannot be trusted to do the right thing on their own, how would the situation be improved by taking a subset of those very same careless, stupid and malicious human beings and giving them societal permission to forcibly control all the others?

– Larken Rose, *The Most Dangerous Superstition*

Perhaps most telling is that if you suggest to the average person that maybe God does not exist, he will likely respond with less emotion and hostility than if you bring up the idea of life without "government." This indicates which religion people are more deeply emotionally attached to, and which religion they actually believe in more firmly. In fact, they believe so deeply in "government" that they do not even recognize it as being a belief at all.

– Larken Rose, *The Most Dangerous Superstition*

If, for example, someone has a "right" to housing, and housing comes only from the knowledge, skills and efforts of other people, it means that one person has the right to force another person to build him a house.

– Larken Rose, *The Most Dangerous Superstition*

...[W]e now have the first complete data set of all suicide terrorist attacks around the world from 1980 to 2009... research on who becomes a suicide terrorist showed that virtually none could be diagnosed as mentally ill, while many were religious and, most striking, nearly all emerged from communities resisting foreign military occupation... From 1980 to 2003, there were 345 completed suicide terrorist attacks by 524 suicide terrorists who actually killed themselves on a mission to kill others, half of whom are secular. The world leader was the Tamil Tigers (a secular, Hindu group) who carried out more attacks than Hamas or Palestinian Islamic Jihad (PIJ) during this period. Further, at least a third of the suicide attacks in predominantly Muslim countries were carried out by secular terrorist groups, such as the Kurdistan Workers Party (PKK) in Turkey. Instead of religion, what over 95% of all suicide terrorist attacks before 2004 had in common was a strategic goal: to compel a democratic state to withdraw combat forces that are threatening territory that the terrorists' prize. From Lebanon to Sri Lanka to the West Bank to Chechnya, the central goal of every suicide terrorist campaign has been to resist military occupation by a democracy.... It was the Hindu, avowedly antireligious Liberation Tigers of Tamil Eelam (LTTE) in Sri Lanka, whose 157 suicide terrorists totaled more than Hamas and all other Palestinian suicide groups combined. Of the Palestinian suicide terrorists, more than a third were from secular groups, such as the Al-Aqsa Martyrs' Brigade and the Popular Front for the Liberation of Palestine (PFLP). Of the suicide terrorists associated with Hezbollah in Lebanon during the 1980s, only 21% were Islamic fundamentalists while 71% were communists and socialists; 8% were Christians. In Turkey, 100% of the PKK's suicide attackers were secular. Overall, Islamic fundamentalism cannot account for over half of the known affiliations of the 524 total suicide terrorists from 1980 to 2003 — 184 were from Islamic fundamentalist groups (35% comprising 73 Al Qaeda, 5 Lebanese, 5 Kashmiri Rebels, 69 Hamas, 34 Palestinian Islamic Jihad) and 236 from secular groups (45% comprising 157 Tamil Tigers, 42 Al-Aqsa, 22 Lebanese, 15 PKK), while 12 (21%) had unknown ideological affiliations.... Further, notice that there are no suicide attackers from Iran — one of the largest Islamic fundamentalist populations in the world, with a population greater than Iraq, Saudi Arabia, Kuwait, Jordan, and Syria combined.

– Robert Pape and James K. Feldman, Cutting the Fuse

Then the fighters realized that the gang in the White House could not see things clearly, and that their leader (that idiot they obey) was claiming that we envied their lifestyle — when the truth, which this Pharaoh would like to hide — is that **we are attacking them because of their injustice toward the Muslim world, and especially Palestine and Iraq, as well as their occupation of the land of the two sanctuaries.** When the fighters saw this, they decided to come out of the shadows and take the fight into their territory, into their homes.

– Osama bin Laden,
in (Eds.) Kepel and Milelli, Al Qaeda in Its Own Words,
translated by Pascale Ghazaleh

The human tragedy reaches its climax in the fact that after all the exertions and sacrifices of hundreds of millions of people and the victories of the Righteous Cause we have still not found Peace or Security, and that we lie in the grip of even worse perils than those we have surmounted.

– Winston Churchill, *The Gathering Storm*

Media pundits have been gushing over Biden's alleged accomplishment, but less than one year ago, on August 29, 2021, also in Kabul, **ten entirely innocent civilians** were destroyed by a U.S. drone strike on the basis of "evidence" that the target was driving a white Toyota Corolla and seemed to be acting "suspiciously."

– Laurie Calhoun, Author of *We Kill Because We Can*

After America emerged as the undisputed leader of the West in 1945, however, the shocks, reversals, and humiliations at the hands of Stalin were greater than those that had caused Britain to declare war in 1939. America, however, chose a different course. Embracing the wisdom of George Kennan, America pursued a policy of containment and conscious avoidance of a Third World War.

When Stalin trashed the Yalta agreement, terrorizing the peoples of **Poland** and Eastern Europe for whom Britain had gone to war, America was stunned and sickened but issued no ultimata. When Moscow blockaded Berlin in violation of Allied rights, Truman responded with an airlift, not armored divisions or atom bombs.

When Stalin's agents carried out the **Prague coup in 1948**, Truman did not see in Czechoslovakia an issue that justified war, as Churchill had when the Czechs were forced to give up the Sudetenland. America's answer was NATO, drawing a red line across Europe that the West could defend, as Britain should have done in March 1939, instead of handing out the insane war guarantee to Poland. And where the British had failed to line up a Russian alliance before giving its war guarantee, America enlisted ten European allies before committing herself to defend West Germany.

Unlike Churchill in the 1930s, American leaders of the late 1940s and 1950s believed that, while the fate of Poland and Czechoslovakia was tragic, both were beyond any U.S. vital interest. From 1949 to 1989, the American army never crossed the Yalta line. When East Germans rose in **1953** and Hungarians in **1956**, Eisenhower declined to act. In 1959, Ike welcomed the "Butcher of Budapest" to Camp David. When Khrushchev built the Berlin Wall, Kennedy called up the reserves, then sent them home after a year. In the missile crisis of **1962**, Kennedy cut a secret deal to take U.S. missiles out of Turkey for Khrushchev's taking Russian missiles out of Cuba. When the Prague Spring was crushed in **1968**, LBJ did nothing. U.S. inaction was not due to cowardice but cold calculation as to what was worth risking war with a nuclear-armed Soviet Union and what was not worth risking war. When the Polish workers' movement, Solidarity, was crushed in **1981**, Ronald Reagan denounced the repression but he neither broke diplomatic relations with Warsaw nor imposed economic sanctions.

Eisenhower and Reagan were not Chamberlains, but neither were they Churchills. Who ruled in the capitals east of the Elbe was not to them a vital U.S. interest worth a war.

– Patrick J. Buchanan, *Churchill, Hitler, and the Unnecessary War*

Drone strikes conducted by the United States during a 5-month-long campaign in Afghanistan caused the deaths of unintended targets nearly nine out of ten times, leaked intelligence documents suggest.

The apparent 10 percent success rate with regards to a specific span in America's drone war is among the most damning revelations to surface so far as the result of a series of articles published by The Intercept on Thursday this week which rely on classified and confidential intelligence documents supplied by an unknown source.

Obama-led drone strikes kill innocents 90% of the time.

– *Washington Times*, October (2015)

This is capitalism's trump card. It encourages creativity and empathy, and puts them at the service of the wants and needs of the people. The inequality the socialist left despises, isn't created by the entrepreneur. It's created by us. The proud boast of Democratic socialism is that it puts the people in charge of the economy. What control do you have over the post office or the DMV? We vote in elections every two or four years, but as consumers we exercise our choices daily, directly through the market. The free market is far more reflective of popular consent, than democratic socialism. We don't have to extend democracy from the political to the economic sphere, because we already have it. Capitalism, not socialism, is the true form of social justice.

– Dinesh D'Souza, *Trump Card: Beating Socialism,*
Corruption and the Deep State

The annual cost of federal regulations in the United States increased to more than $1.75 trillion in 2008. Had every U.S. household paid an equal share of the federal regulatory burden, each would have owed $15,586 in 2008. By comparison, the federal regulatory burden exceeds by 50 percent private spending on health care, which equaled $10,500 per household in 2008. While all citizens and businesses pay some portion of these costs, the distribution of the burden of regulations is quite uneven. The portion of regulatory costs that falls initially on businesses was $8,086 per employee in 2008. Small businesses, defined as firms employing fewer than 20 employees, bear the largest burden of federal regulations. As of 2008, small businesses face an annual regulatory cost of $10,585 per employee, which is 36 percent higher than the regulatory cost facing large firms (defined as firms with 500 or more employees).

– Nicole V. Crain and W. Mark Crain,
"The Impact of Regulatory Costs on Small Firms"

The Economic Legacy of Slavery

What was accomplished by the enslavement of untold millions of human beings in countries around the world?

No doubt particular projects here and there were the fruits of slave labor, but it would be difficult to make the more general case that slavery advanced the economic level of those societies in which it existed on a mass scale.

The American South, for example, was by no means the most economically dynamic region of the country, either during or after the era of slavery. It was in fact the poorest. Brazil, which imported several times as many slaves as the United States, remained a relatively backward country until the large-scale European immigration that began after the era of slavery was over. The slave societies of North Africa and the Middle East, which absorbed even more millions of slaves than the Western Hemisphere, lagged conspicuously behind the technological and economic level of the West, both during and after the end of slavery — until oil, not slaves, raised their standards of living in the modern era. In Europe, it was the nations in the Western region of the continent, where slavery was abolished first, that led the continent and the world into the modern industrial age.

In many parts of the world, slaves were luxuries, or at least domestic amenities, rather than capital investments intended to yield a profit. A large retinue of slaves was a display of wealth and power, whether in Ancient Rome, China, Africa, Thailand, Tibet, or elsewhere. In regions where slaves were part of a lifestyle — and this included much of the Islamic world — it can hardly be surprising that slavery did not create any notable economic development. That was not its role. Moreover, even in societies where slaves were intended to produce profits for slave owners, it is by no means apparent that those profits played any major role beyond the current consumption of those slave owners.

– Thomas Sowell, *Race and Culture*

The problem is this: every flaw in consumers is worse in voters. You might object, "That's obvious; they are the same people!" That's exactly the point that advocates for government corrections of market failure are missing, folks. In artificial laboratory settings, and sometimes in real-world choice settings, people are bad at making decisions. But they are better at choosing in markets, where they have prices and brand names, than those same people trying to choose in democratic political settings, where advertising is intentionally misleading and party brand names are almost meaningless.

– Michael Munger, *Every Flaw in Consumers
Is Worse in Voters, Part Deux*

So, this is the essential paradox of regulation: To favor increasing regulation, you have to think the unorganized mass of consumers, taxpayers, and common public will generally be more effective in lobbying for their interests than organized, highly motivated special interest groups who keep offices in Washington, D.C. You have to think that the people who enjoy concentrated benefits and can spread their costs onto others will be less effective than the masses who suffer from diffused costs.

– Jason Brennan, *Why It's OK to Want to Be Rich*

Our schools provide many hours of lessons on climate change, but I wonder how many teachers, let alone pupils, are aware that **climate-related deaths have decreased by as much as 97 per cent over the past 100 years**, as the OFDA / CRED data show.

– "Why don't we ever hear the good news about climate?"
Spiked.com, January 9, 2023.

We're vulnerable to politically motivated reasoning: the (unconscious) goal of our political deliberation is not to find the truth but rather to protect our identity as a loyal member of our political "team" — Democrat, Republican, libertarian, socialist, and so on. We are distressingly good at dismissing, downgrading, and explaining away evidence that indicates we're on the wrong side of the political aisle.

– Christopher Freiman, *Why It's OK to Ignore Politics*

"Without a state," we read, Somalia under statelessness descended into a Hobbesian "state of nature where life is nasty, brutish, and short."

Then, after two whole paragraphs on the situation in Somalia, we get study questions. If you look *really, really closely*, you may detect *a very slight bias* in these questions.

VERY SLIGHT, I tell you.

> "1. Which is preferable, bad government or no government?

> "2. Why hasn't Somalia without a state become the paradise that libertarians anticipate?"

Now for one thing, was there ever a libertarian who predicted that a stateless Somalia — or a stateless anywhere else — would be a "paradise"?

More importantly, if we're going to get a picture that's worth anything of life in Somalia without the state, the correct comparison to make is not between Somalia and the United States (the comparison most writers like this are implicitly making), but between Somalia and comparable African countries.

And on that front, Somalia during its stateless period comes out pretty darn well. In most metrics of living standards it held steady or improved.

In the *Journal of Economic Behavior & Organization* in 2008, Professor Benjamin Powell and his colleagues wrote:

> This paper's main contribution to the literature has been to compare Somalia's living standards to those of 41 other sub-Saharan African countries both before and after the collapse of the national government. We find that Somalia's living standards have generally improved and that they compare relatively favorably with many existing African states. Importantly, we find that Somali living standards have often improved, not just in absolute terms, but also relative to other African countries since the collapse of the Somali central government.

Economist Peter Leeson (in *Anarchy Unbound*, Cambridge University Press), reports similar findings — yes, Somalia ranked low in some categories during the stateless period, but that's where it ranked before statelessness, too, and if anything it actually made progress in those categories (life expectancy was up, for instance, and infant mortality was down).

– Thomas E. Woods, Jr.

There's plenty to say regarding Sweden: (1) its "socialist" policies were made possible by wealth created under an essentially capitalist economy (as recently as the 1950s, remember, government spent less as a percentage of GDP in Sweden than in the U.S.); (2) Swedes earn about 50 percent more in the U.S., in our supposedly wicked economy; and (3) since Sweden's explosion of social welfare spending there have been zero jobs created on net in the private sector.

– Thomas E. Woods, Jr.

The funny thing is that if the Sanderses and Ocasio-Cortezes of the world made the U.S. more like Sweden, what would really happen? They haven't updated their perception of Sweden and if the U.S. became more like us, the United States would have to have more free markets, more free trade, pension reform with private accounts, a national school voucher system with freedom of choice and public funding going to private schools as well, low corporate taxes and no taxes on wealth, property and inheritance. Be careful what you wish for.

– Johan Norberg, *Lessons from Sweden*

If men were like ants, there would be no interest in human freedom. If individual men, like ants, were uniform, interchangeable, devoid of specific personality traits of their own, then who would care whether they were free or not? Who, indeed, would care if they lived or died? The glory of the human race is the uniqueness of each individual, the fact that every person, though similar in many ways to others, possesses a completely individuated personality of his own. It is the fact of each person's uniqueness — the fact that no two people can be wholly interchangeable — that makes each and every man irreplaceable and that makes us care whether he lives or dies, whether he is happy or oppressed. And, finally, it is the fact that these unique personalities need freedom for their full development that constitutes one of the major arguments for a free society.

– Murray N. Rothbard, *Egalitarianism as Revolt Against Nature*

The most immediate effect of licensing is to restrict the number of practitioners because of the higher entry costs involved in meeting the qualifications of the activity. Some licenses, as in the cases of cosmeticians and barbers, require many months of schooling. Others require the installation of costly health and safety equipment. Still others demand the purchase of the license or "certificate of authorization" from an incumbent practitioner that can cost millions of dollars, as was the case when interstate trucking was highly regulated. Further, some jurisdictions issue only a fixed number of licenses or authorizations. All of these requirements raise the cost of entry, which naturally leads to a smaller number of practitioners.

Restricting that number is only the initial effect of licensing. A secondary effect is that the price of the good or service offered is higher than it would otherwise be. The result of restricting entry to a business or occupation, and probably the primary intent of licensing, is to raise the incomes of incumbent practitioners. Evidence supports this self-interested behavior: (1) most licensure laws are the result of intense lobbying by incumbents, not of consumers demanding more protection from incompetent or unscrupulous practitioners; (2) when incumbents in an unlicensed trade lobby for licensing (or when those in one already licensed lobby for higher entry requirements) they virtually always seek a "grandfather" clause that exempts them from meeting the new requirements, leaving the burden of the higher entry costs to be borne mainly by new entrants; (3) practitioner violations of the licensing codes, such as price-cutting and extra hours, are nearly always reported to the licensing board by the incumbents rather than by customers.

– Walter E. Williams, *Race and Economics*

By contrast, those who are promoting process goals are seeking to have incremental trade-offs made by individuals directly experiencing both the benefits and the costs of their own decisions. Those who are promoting outcome goals are seeking to create categorical priorities chosen by third parties, and imposed by government compulsion on those who directly experience both the benefits and the costs...

Is it of no consequence if everyone's income, education and life expectancy double over some span of time, even if that necessarily increases the gaps? Why should eliminating gaps be the goal when different individuals and groups do not want the same things, or do not have the same priorities or urgencies about these gaps?...

People who depict markets as cold, impersonal institutions, and their own notions as humane and compassionate, have it directly backwards. It is when people make their own economic decisions, taking into account costs that matter to themselves, and known only to themselves, that this knowledge becomes part of the trade-offs they choose, whether as consumers or producers.

– Thomas Sowell, *Discrimination and Disparities*

Euphemisms are another form of insinuation that enables ideas to bypass factual or analytical tests. When John Rawls in his *A Theory of Justice* repeatedly referred to outcomes that "society" can "arrange," these euphemisms finessed aside the plain fact that only government has the power to override millions of people's mutually agreed transactions terms. Interior decorators arrange. Governments compel. It is not a subtle distinction. Nor is Rawls the only income redistributionist to evade the reality of compulsion — which is to say, the loss of millions of people's freedom to make their own decisions about their own lives, when an inequality of economic outcomes is replaced by a far more dangerous increased inequality of power.

– Thomas Sowell, *Discrimination and Disparities*

Serious empirical analyses done by everyone from myself to the Manhattan Institute's Heather Mac Donald to www.killedbypolice.net — an entire web resource set up to study this topic — invariably conclude that fewer than 1,200 people of all races and sexes are killed annually by American police officers. In a typical year, such as the representative year of 2015, roughly 250 (258) of these people will be Black. It is true that the Black percentage of the individuals killed by police, 22–24 percent, is slightly higher than the 13–14 percent representation of Blacks in the overall U.S. population. However, this roughly 10 percent gap is wholly explained by the fact that the Black crime rate, violent crime rate, arrest rate, and police encounter rate are all significantly higher than the equivalent rates for Whites. There is no evidence for any of Black Lives Matter's major claims.

– Wilfred Reilly, *Taboo: 10 Facts You Can't Talk About*

Rather than picking between two racialist sides and fighting for one or the other, American citizens can simply begin telling the truth about race relations. There is no race war going on in the U.S.A., and there certainly is no epidemic of White on-Black crime. In fact, interracial crimes on an annual basis have been consistently 75–85 percent Black-on-White for the past thirty years. More importantly, there is no horrifying epidemic of interracial crimes of any variety because 84 percent of White murder victims and 93 percent of Black murder victims are killed by a mundane member of their own race. We see constant media coverage of BBQ Becky, Permit Patty, Coupon Carl, and George Zimmerman not because these people are everywhere, but because the corporate media have an agenda to push. We should stop taking this agenda seriously — today.

– Wilfred Reilly, *Taboo: 10 Facts You Can't Talk About*

The main points of the last two chapters were that cultural differences between groups (1) exist and (2) predict success. A corollary to these points is that, when all cultural differences are adjusted for, contemporary racism has almost nothing to do with the major problems faced by minority

Americans today. This is, of course, a wildly provocative statement. The idea that the United States today is an "institutionally" or "structurally" prejudiced society is a cornerstone of modern liberal thought. The Black Lives Matter movement alone has staged 2,406 major marches against racism during the past few years. However, any serious claim that contemporary or recent bigotry is the cause of phenomena such as the 75 percent Black illegitimacy rate founders on three rocks. First, these problems did not exist among Blacks (or anyone else) when racism was much worse, (2) these problems do not exist for successful, dark-skinned African and Asian immigrants to the U.S.A., and (3) many or most such problems do exist among poor Whites — perhaps the most genuinely neglected group in America — to roughly the same extent that they do among Blacks.

– Wilfred Reilly, *Taboo: 10 Facts You Can't Talk About*

Imagine Virtuous Vani cares deeply about others and is willing to do whatever it takes to save lives. She believes that processed sugar is a scourge killing Americans. So one day she packs a pistol, invades the local 7-Eleven, and declares, "This here gun says you can't sell Big Gulps anymore."

Principled Peter believes that you don't give enough money to charity. You're living high while people die. One day he sends you an email: "FYI: I hacked into your bank account. I transferred a third of it to poor single moms."

Decent Dani thinks you should buy American rather than German cars. After all, your fellow citizens provide you with roads, schools, and police. You owe them some business. He finds you shopping at a foreign dealer, pulls out a Taser, and says, "You know what? I'll let you buy that BMW, but only if you first pay me $3,000."

You'd probably regard Vani, Peter, and Dani as criminals. How dare they treat you like that? You'd want the police to arrest them.

But there's a puzzle here. While the police would indeed arrest Vani, Peter, and Dani, they're also happy to help other people — bureaucrats in Washington, Berlin, or Ottawa — do the same things Vani, Peter, and Dani want to do. So this set of examples suggests a few questions: What, if anything, explains why it's wrong for Peter to take a third of your income but not wrong for the government tax office to do so? What, if anything, justifies the Food and Drug Administration in determining what you can and can't eat but forbids Vani from doing so? In general, governments claim the right to do things ordinary people may not do. What, if anything, justifies that?

This is one of the central questions in political philosophy.

– Jason Brennan, *Political Philosophy: An Introduction*

For people seeking facts, rather than political or ideological goals, there are many factual tests that might be applied, in order to see if the wealth of the wealthy is derived from the poverty of the poor. One way might be to see if countries with many billionaires — either absolutely or relative to the size of the population — have higher or lower standards of living among the rest of their people. The United States, for example, has more billionaires than there are in the entire continent of Africa plus the Middle East. But even Americans living in conditions officially defined as poverty usually have a higher standard of living than that of most of the people in Africa and the Middle East.

Thomas Sowell, *Social Justice Fallacies*

[L]eftists (the ones who are anti-state but also support social safety nets) could have most everything they want in an anarchist society in the form of mutual aid societies. Those are the types of leftists that are worth reaching out to.

– Ace Archist

Afterword

I always admired Progressives' unapologetic opposition to unjust ideas. Progressives could correctly identify unjust ways of operating society. But today, whether it is colonialism, racism, sexism, classism, xenophobia, or the military-industrial complex, Progressives have embraced all of those vicious ideas and have made them the center of their campaigns.

They explicitly embrace colonialism by supporting the federal government's centralization of control. They judge people by race, gender, and class. They negatively generalize "stupid Americans" and "evil Russian interferers" at every opportunity, and wish for the state to have more money and power knowing that a large portion of that money and power will be directed to military-industrial interests, leading to the mass murder of innocent human beings.

Progressivism survives by only looking at one side of the equation when it comes to social and economic issues. They see the large amounts of revenue that organizations like Amazon have, and conclude that Amazon must be vilified. They seldom if ever ask: Why do so many people voluntarily choose to spend their scarce money in exchange for so many Amazon products? How many people with lower incomes have had greater access to products as a result of Amazon's services? Thanks to Amazon, how many more options does the average person have to choose from just by scrolling on his phone or computer? How many authors and small businesses are empowered by Amazon Marketplace, instead of having to go through a major publishing house or having to open up their own warehouse?

It's common to see Progressives — who offer me no job, no products, and no services — claim that my real enemies are people who voluntarily offer me those things. Like a jealous spouse, they become abusive when they feel insecure, rather than do the work that it takes to improve themselves. It's noteworthy that Amazon has voluntarily chosen to enact a $15-an-hour minimum wage, the very thing Progressives say only can be achieved via state coercion.[61]

Zero-sum thinking is defined as situations in which "one person's gain would be another's loss." If Progressives could clearly differentiate between mutually beneficial exchanges and coercive, parasitic transactions, they would cease to be Progressives.

Unable to move beyond zero-sum thinking, Progressives will abandon any sense of gratitude for the society around them, making it highly improbable that they will be able to test theories empirically about what makes societies thrive and which policies or institutions lead to the impoverishment of society.

Progressives should appreciate that genius comes in many different forms. Socrates, Leonardo DiCaprio, Dave Chappelle, Michelangelo, and Nikola Tesla were all geniuses. Genius also comes in the form of ideas regarding how to innovate and produce things which people want, and to do so in an affordable way so that the products can be accessible to the masses.

Progressives' making enemies of the great voluntary innovators in society is not just unnecessarily divisive; it stops the rest of us from having access to the fruits of those innovators' talents.

Looking at the monarchical systems of the past, many intellectuals incorrectly blamed the shortcomings of said monarchies on the elitist, arbitrary characteristics of the kings and queens who flaunted their royalty while others lived in poverty.

The problem with monarchy is not elitism or some people having a huge sway in society. As the Iron Law of Oligarchy teaches us, any time people organize, a very small portion of them will have most of the power and influence. The problem with monarchy lies in the fact that one organization — the state — has an exemption from morality by having a monopoly on violence within a geographical area. The government has a recognized right to perform actions (impose taxes, regulations, and declare wars) that would clearly be seen as criminal if any other organization engaged in them.

Imagine the Catholic Church (or any person or group of people) doing what the state does every day:

> Everyone who doesn't give the Catholic Church 25% of his annual income every year will be put in jail. If he resists the Jesuit officer, the officer has the right to shoot him. Everyone by law must contribute to the Catholic Church School Fund, and if parents don't send their kids there, they will be jailed for a truancy law violation. Most people need a license by force of law from the Catholic Church in order to work; this way the Church can keep you and other customers safe. And all humans have a nine-digit Catholic Security Number so the Church knows who's who. If the Catholic Church decides to wage war on the Church of Scientology, everyone must be forced to fund

the war, and men ages 18–45 will be conscripted to perform forced labor against their will.

The problem with this situation is not that we don't get to vote on who the Pope is once every four years, or that the votes need accurate counting; it's that some people claim an exemption from common-sense morality by engaging in nonconsensual activity.

The solution is to decriminalize all capitalist acts between consenting adults and cease to have moral double standards for elites and laymen. True empowerment of the economically vulnerable comes from economic freedom, not from getting to choose which politician gets your one vote every few years.

In short, privatize *everything*. Incentives of profit and loss allow you to harmonize individual self-interest with collective well-being. The free market approach is the only morally justified system, since it relies on voluntaryism while recognizing the right of self-defense.

Appendix: The Nonexistent Difference Between National Socialism and Democratic Socialism

National Socialism and Democratic Socialism both advocate institutionalized violence by the state against peaceful people. They differ only in terms of rhetoric.

The most popular self-described Democratic Socialists in America today are Senator Bernie Sanders and Congresswoman Alexandria Ocasio-Cortez. Although Americans account for roughly 5% of the global population, these candidates focus primarily on American well-being at the expense of the other 95% of human beings.

Is it because Americans are the poorest people on Earth in need of the most help? Hardly — most Americans today have access to products and services the wealthiest people in history never had access to.

If they opposed Nationalism and supported Democracy, they would spend more time drafting policy proposals for the 1.4 billion Chinese, 1.4 billion Indians, and 1.2 billion Africans. Their rhetoric (along with that of every single American Democratic Socialist I have ever met) betrays the reality that they too care mostly about their own "nation" and are therefore Nationalists.

Nothing wrong with that. But the sanctimonious dismissal Democratic Socialists have of people who are proud of their country drives me up the wall. They tell us that loving your country is wrong, unless you live in Ukraine as of 2022. They tell us that you cannot take pride in your ancestors' accomplishments, but you must forever pay for their sins via reparations and harassment by academics. They tell us that imperialism is bad, and yet all 330 million Americans across 50 states must obey Washington, D.C., and that everyone who supports secession is basically Jefferson Davis.

Both National and Democratic Socialists support the following:

- The existence of a state apparatus which has a legal monopoly on the right to initiate violence against peaceful people (i.e., government supremacy).

- The state monopolizing the money supply (i.e., the central bank).

• State compulsory education.

• State regulation of economic activity between consenting adults.

• Antitrust laws.

• Commercial and occupational licensing.

• Higher taxes on "the rich."

• Tariffs.

• Immigration restrictions.

• Both constantly vilify "the banks and big business" (see the National Socialists' 25-Point Program).

• Taxation, or the right of the state to collect its funding in a coercive manner, which no other group has the right to do.

• State police (which is why "Defund the Police" was clearly a scam, as they know that the state needs police to enforce the regulations and taxes which they wish to impose on us).

• State military apparatus (not something every country has — for instance, Liechtenstein).

• Judging people explicitly by their race.

There are two ways to achieve your ends in life: either through mutually beneficial, *voluntary* exchanges, or through acts of *violence* or threats thereof. Both types of socialists seek to control hundreds of millions of strangers under the guise of "helping."

Acknowledgments

I am forever indebted to Dr. Christopher Freiman and Dr. Jason Brennan for taking the time to come on to the Libertarian Institute podcast and discuss vitally important topics with a college dropout. Throughout this book, I tried to articulate my understanding of the lessons they taught me in the hope that more people would be introduced to these ideas.

Thanks to Scott Horton and all of my colleagues at the Libertarian Institute for passionately speaking truth, regardless of popularity.

Thanks to Tom Woods for leading by example.

Thanks to Bob Murphy for his economic wisdom.

Thanks to Dave Smith for unapologetically spreading the message of freedom.

Many thanks as well to my copyeditor Ben Parker.

Thanks also to Mike Dworski for his assistance in preparing this book for publication.

Thanks to Andrew Zehnder for designing the front and back cover.

And thanks, as always, to all listeners of the *Don't Tread on Anyone* podcast.

The Libertarian Institute

Check out the Libertarian Institute at LibertarianInstitute.org. It's Scott Horton, Sheldon Richman, Laurie Calhoun, James Bovard, Kyle Anzalone, Connor Freeman, Keith Knight, Tommy Salmons and the best libertarian writers and podcast hosts on the Internet. We are a 501(c)(3) tax-exempt charitable organization. EIN 83-2869616.

Help support our efforts — including our project to purchase wholesale copies of this book to send to important congressmen and women, antiwar groups and influential people in the media. We don't have a big marketing department to push this effort. We need your help to do it. And thank you.

LibertarianInstitute.org/donate or
The Libertarian Institute
612 W. 34th St.
Austin, TX 78705

Check out all of our other great books at LibertarianInstitute.org/books:
Hotter Than the Sun: Time to Abolish Nuclear Weapons by Scott Horton
Enough Already: Time to End the War on Terrorism by Scott Horton
Fool's Errand: Time to End the War in Afghanistan by Scott Horton
Diary of a Psychosis: How Public Health Disgraced Itself During Covid Mania by Thomas E. Woods, Jr.
Last Rights: The Death of American Liberty by James Bovard
Questioning the COVID Company Line: Critical Thinking in Hysterical Times by Laurie Calhoun
Voluntaryist Handbook by Keith Knight
The Fake China Threat and Its Very Real Danger by Joseph Solis-Mullen
The Great Ron Paul: The Scott Horton Show Interviews 2004–2019
No Quarter: The Ravings of William Norman Grigg, edited by Tom Eddlem
Coming to Palestine by Sheldon Richman
What Social Animals Owe to Each Other by Sheldon Richman

Keep a look out for more great titles to be published in 2023 and 2024.

Endnotes

[1] Edward Stringham, *Anarchy and the Law: The Political Economy of Choice* (New Brunswick: Transaction Publishers, 2011).

[2] "'When I See Racial Disparities, I See Racism.' Discussing Race, Gender and Mobility," *New York Times*, March 27, 2018. nytimes.com/interactive/2018/03/27/upshot/reader-questions-about-race-gender-and-mobility.html.

[3] Daniel Larison, "Republican Presidents Never Reduce the Size of Government," *The American Conservative*, March 6, 2012. theamericanconservative.com/republican-presidents-never-reduce-the-size-of-government.

[4] Glenn Greenwald, "The Enduring False Narrative about the Pulse Massacre Shows the Power of Media Propaganda," June 14, 2021. greenwald.substack.com/p/the-enduring-false-narrative-about.

[5] "President Obama on the Tragic Shooting in Orlando," White House, June 16, 2016. obamawhitehouse.archives.gov/blog/2016/06/12/president-obama-tragic-shooting-orlando.

[6] Monivette Cordeiro, "City releases transcripts of 911 calls between Pulse gunman and negotiator," *Orlando Weekly*, September 23, 2016. orlandoweekly.com/news/city-releases-transcripts-of-911-calls-between-pulse-gunman-and-negotiator-2527992.

[7] Micah Zenko and Jennifer Wilson, "How Many Bombs Did the United States Drop in 2016?" Council on Foreign Relations, January 5, 2017. cfr.org/blog/how-many-bombs-did-united-states-drop-2016.

[8] Tami Luhby and Christopher Hickey, "U.S. Black-White Inequality in 4 Charts," CNN, June 1, 2021. cnn.com/2021/06/01/politics/black-white-racial-wealth-gap/index.html.

[9] Neeraj Shetty (@NeerajShetty): "This is amazing @AOC! I don't see a future where gender pay gap exists. It should end right now!" August 30, 2019. twitter.com/NeerajShetty/Status/1167325816599896066.

[10] "Time Spent Working by Full- and Part-Time Status, Gender, and Location in 2014," *The Economics Daily*, U.S. Bureau of Labor Statistics, July 2, 2015. bls.gov/opub/ted/2015/time-spent-working-by-full-and-part-time-status-gender-and-location-in-2014.htm.

[11] Silbey, Susan. "Why Do So Many Women Who Study Engineering Leave the Field?" *Harvard Business Review.* August 23, 2016. hbr.org/2016/08/why-do-so-many-women-who-study-engineering-leave-the-field.

[12] "Study: Black Immigrants Earn More than U.S.-Born Blacks," Black Enterprise, September 24, 2015. blackenterprise.com/tag/black-immigrants.

[13] Abbigail J. Chiodo and Michael T. Owyang, "For Love or Money: Why Married Men Make More," Federal Reserve Bank of St. Louis, April 1, 2002. stlouisfed.org/publications/regional-economist/april-2002/for-love-or-money-why-married-men-make-more.

[14] René Bennett. "U.S. Household Income by Age, Gender, Education and More," Bankrate, February 11, 2022. bankrate.com/personal-finance/median-salary-by-age.

[15] "Average Income by Age plus Median, Top 1%, and All Income Percentiles," DQYDJ (Don't Quit Your Day Job), November 16, 2022. dqydj.com/average-median-top-income-by-age-percentiles.

[16] "AAPI Demographics: Data on Asian American Ethnicities, Geography, Income, and Education," USAFacts, May 1, 2023. usafacts.org/articles/the-diverse-demographics-of-asian-americans.

[17] "Demographic Data Project: Gender and Individual Homelessness," National Alliance to End Homelessness, n.d. endhomelessness.org/demographic-data-project-gender-and-individual-homelessness.

[18] DeVore, Chuck. "Fatal Employment: Men 10 Times More Likely than Women to Be Killed at Work" *Forbes*, December 19, 2018. forbes.com/sites/chuckdevore/2018/12/19/fatal-employment-men-10-times-more-likely-than-women-to-be-killed-at-work/?sh=21a5b53152e8.

[19] The Washington Post. "Every Fatal Police Shooting since 2015," *Washington Post*, 2022. washingtonpost.com/graphics/investigations/police-shootings-database.

[20] "Who Are the Nation's 4 Million Teachers?" USAFacts. December 4, 2020. usafacts.org/articles/who-are-the-nations-4m-teachers.

[21] "The Most Surprising OnlyFans Gender Statistics and Trends in 2023," Gitnux, March 21, 2023. blog.gitnux.com/onlyfans-gender-statistics.

[22] "NPR Choice Page," npr.org, 2019. npr.org/sections/parallels/2013/11/01/241895965/how-one-kenyan-tribe-produces-the-worlds-best-runners.

[23] Isaiah Reynolds. "Your Doughnut Box Is Pink Thanks to Cambodian Refugees," *Business Insider*, June 10, 2023. insider.com/pink-doughnut-box-cambodian-refugees-donut-king-2023-6.

[24] Mark J. Perry, "*Fortune* 500 Firms 1955 v. 2016: Only 12% Remain, Thanks to the Creative Destruction That Fuels Economic Prosperity," American Enterprise Institute, December 13, 2016. aei.org/carpe-diem/fortune-500-firms-1955-v-2016-only-12-remain-thanks-to-the-creative-destruction-that-fuels-economic-prosperity.

[25] "Declassified Memorandum: The Decline and Fall of Castro," U.S. Department of State, April 6, 1960. nsarchive.gwu.edu/document/27400-document-1-state-department-memorandum-decline-and-fall-castro-secret-april-6-1960.

[26] "The Southern Argument for Slavery," UShistory.org, Independence Hall Association in Philadelphia, n.d. ushistory.org/us/27f.asp?source=post_page.

[27] Billy Binion, "They Fell Behind on Their Property Taxes. So the Government Sold Their Homes — and Kept the Profits," *Reason*, January 17, 2023. reason.com/2023/01/17/they-fell-behind-on-their-property-taxes-so-the-government-sold-their-homes-and-kept-the-profits.

[28] CFI Team, "Public Goods," Corporate Finance Institute, n.d. corporatefinanceinstitute.com/resources/economics/public-goods.

[29] Christopher Freiman, *Unequivocal Justice: Political Philosophy for the Real World* (Abingdon: Routledge, 2017).

[30] "Good News in History September 20," Good News Network, September 20, 2023. goodnewsnetwork.org/events060920.

[31] "Raising Funds for Liberty," National Park Service. nps.gov/museum/exhibits/statue_liberty/raising_funds.html.

[32] Alexandria Ocasio-Cortez (@AOC): "It is utterly embarrassing that 'pay people enough to live' is a stance that's even up for debate. Override the parliamentarian and raise the wage…" March 2, 2021. twitter.com/AOC/Status/1366922134057058304?Ref_src=Twsrc%255Etfw.

[33] "Kennedy Responds to Wal-Mart's Call for Minimum Wage Increase," U.S. Senate Committee on Health, Education, Labor & Pensions, October 25, 2005. help.senate.gov/ranking/newsroom/press/kennedy-responds-to-wal-marts-call-for-minimum-wage-increase.

[34] "Walmart's CEO Asks Congress to Boost Federal Minimum Wage Amid Criticism for Its Own Pay Policies," *Money*, June 6, 2019. money.com/walmart-ceo-minimum-wage.

[35] Milton Friedman and Rose Friedman, *Free to Choose: A Personal Statement* (New York: Harcourt Brace Jovanovich, 1980), p. 246.

[36] "Characteristics of minimum wage workers, 2021," Bureau of Labor Statistics, April 2022. bls.gov/opub/reports/minimum-wage/2021/home.htm.

37 Nathan Hale and John Leeth, "Evaluating OSHA's Effectiveness and Suggestions for Reform," Mercatus Center, George Washington University, April 23, 2013. mercatus.org/students/research/policy-briefs/evaluating-oshas-effectiveness-and-suggestions-reform.

38 James Tooley and Pauline Dixon, "Private Education is Good for the Poor: A Study of Private Schools Serving the Poor in Low-Income Countries," Cato Institute, December 7, 2005. cato.org/sites/cato.org/files/pubs/pdf/tooley.pdf, p. 53.

39 "Iron Law of Oligarchy," Wikipedia, n.d. en.wikipedia.org/wiki/iron_law_of_oligarchy.

40 Tom Kertscher, "Confiscating U.S. billionaires' wealth would run the U.S. government about 8 months," PolitiFact, November 2, 2021. politifact.com/factchecks/2021/nov/02/viral-image/confiscating-us-billionaires-wealth-would-run-us-g.

41 Todd Krainin, "Jay Austin's Beautiful, Illegal Tiny House," *Reason*, August 9, 2014. reason.com/2014/08/09/jay-austins-beautiful-illegal-tiny-house.

42 Justin Monticello, "This L.A. Musician Built $1,200 Tiny Houses for the Homeless," *Reason*, December 9, 2016. reason.com/podcast/2016/12/09/los-angeles-homeless-tiny-houses.

43 Jordan Betts, "Health Dept. Defends Bleaching Food for Homeless," KSHB 41 Kansas City News, November 5, 2018. kshb.com/news/local-news/kcmo-health-dept-defends-pouring-bleach-on-food-intended-for-homeless.

44 "Horton's Law," Urban Dictionary (user Moa_wearemoa), June 28, 2019. urbandictionary.com/define.php?term=Horton's%20Law.

45 Scott Lincicome, *Empowering the New American Worker: Market-Based Solutions for Today's Workforce* (Washington: Cato Institute, 2023), p. 59.

46 The Hill (@thehill): "Sen. Bernie Sanders: 'What we learned in this election and what we saw every day with our eyes is the incredible degree of voter suppression which exists out there.'" November 21, 2020. Video. twitter.com/thehill/Status/1330356580215185408.

47 "The Federal Budget in Fiscal Year 2022: An Infographic," Congressional Budget Office, U.S. Congress, March 28, 2023. cbo.gov/publication/58888.

48 Corey DeAngelis, "Inflation-Adjusted K-12 Education Spending per Student Has Increased by 280 Percent since 1960," Reason Foundation, June 15, 2020. reason.org/commentary/inflation-adjusted-k-12-education-spending-per-student-has-increased-by-280-percent-since-1960.

49 Walter E. Williams, *Race & Economics: How Much Can Be Blamed on Discrimination?* (Stanford: Hoover Institution Press, 2011).

50 Paul Krugman, *The Conscience of a Liberal* (New York: W.W. Norton & Co., 2009), p. 224.

51 Mark J. Perry, "Chart of the Day… or Century?" American Enterprise Institute, January 17, 2021. aei.org/carpe-diem/chart-of-the-day-or-century-5.

52 Brittany Hunter, "What a Funny Taylor Swift Video Can Teach Us About Health Care," Foundation for Economic Education, October 21, 2019. fee.org/articles/what-a-funny-taylor-swift-video-can-teach-us-about-health-care.

53 Regina Baker, "Why Is the American South Poorer?" WZB, September 18, 2014. wzb.eu/en/events/why-is-the-american-south-poorer.

54 Thomas Sowell, *Black Rednecks and White Liberals* (New York: Encounter Books, 2006).

55 Frederick Douglass, *Narrative of the Life of Frederick Douglass* (New York: Dover Thrift Editions, 2016 [1845]), p. 8.

56 Niall Ferguson, *Civilization: The West and the Rest* (London: Penguin Books, 2012).

57 Amelia Josephson. "The Average Salary by Age in the U.S. — Are You Making What You Should Be?" SmartAsset, June 28, 2018. smartasset.com/retirement/the-average-salary-by-age.

58 Thomas Sowell, *Basic Economics: A Common Sense Guide to the Economy* (New York: Basic Books, 2015 [2000]).

59 Moore, Stephen, *Who's the Fairest of Them All? The Truth About Opportunity, Taxes, and Wealth in America* (New York: Encounter Books, 2012).

60 Ronald Bailey and Marian L. Tupy, *Ten Global Trends Every Smart Person Should Know: And Many Others You Will Find Interesting* (Washington: Cato Institute, 2020), p. 155.

61 "Why Amazon Supports a $15 Minimum Wage," About Amazon, n.d. aboutamazon.com/impact/economy/15-minimum-wage.